THE MAYOR MARRIED WHO?

*A Look at the Lighter Side of a
40-Year Career in City Management*

TIM CASEY

outskirts
press

This book is dedicated to my beautiful wife, Rosalind, daughter Shannon, son-in-law Phil, and our new baby grandson, Rhys Casey Bresnahan.

TABLE OF CONTENTS

INTRODUCTION

WHEN I RETIRED seven years ago, I promised myself that I would write this book when I had some spare time. Well, the opportunity has finally presented itself. The world finds itself in the midst of the 2020 coronavirus (COVID-19) global pandemic, and Roz and I are in our third week of isolation at our Laguna Niguel, California, home.

Worldwide, millions of people have been infected with this novel virus and tens of thousands have perished. Schools and churches are closed, and nonessential businesses are shuttered. Social distancing (i.e., staying at least six feet away from others) and face coverings are the new norm as we are directed to stay in our homes except for necessary trips to the grocery store, pharmacy, or gas station, or to get a little fresh air and outdoor exercise. Millions are temporarily (hopefully) unemployed and the economy is in decline, if not already in recession. Cities and other local governments are scrambling to provide essential services while protecting our democracy through virtual council/board meetings and social media platforms that allow public participation and input from afar.

Fortunately, Roz and I are healthy and hope to stay that way.

Unfortunately, we are not able to visit and hold grandson Rhys until things get back to some kind of normal. We just don't know when that will be. Shannon is our only child, and Rhys is her firstborn and our only grandchild. We hope and pray that the time comes soon for everyone to be together with their families, friends, and loved ones.

Against this unexpected backdrop, the time has come to get this book underway. It is meant to provide a look at the lighter side and some memorable moments of a forty-year career in city management serving four California cities: Manhattan Beach, Ventura, Redondo Beach, and Laguna Niguel. I had the good fortune (i.e., luck) to have been the city manager for thirty-one of those forty years. All of the stories are true and detailed to the best of my sixty-nine-year-old memory. A few names have been changed, but that's all.

I hope you enjoy the read. I know that the memories are going to help me get through these uncertain times.

Chapter 1

MY PUBLIC SERVICE GENES

I'M NOT SURE where my public service genes or roots came from. It may have been my maternal grandfather, Ernest Rupert James, who served in the Missouri State Legislature from 1920 to 1926. It could have been my paternal grandfather, Roy Casey, who worked for the City of Manhattan Beach, California, Water Department for twenty years. His other form of public service was selling illegal alcohol from the back of his fruit-and-vegetable truck on weekends during Prohibition.

My father, Richard Jordan Casey, performed his public service as a navy enlistee during World War II. He interrupted his banking career, served from 1941 to 1945, and was a Pearl Harbor survivor.

However, the real political junkie in the family was my mother, Mary Enid (James) Casey. She loved to listen to the nightly political news (Walter Cronkite was her favorite broadcast journalist), and she looked forward to the weekly arrival of *Time* magazine. If the cover photo was a politician, you could gauge her like or dislike by the way she marked up his or her face with her trusty black felt pen. Mom was a registered Democrat who cared greatly about our government leadership and policies and studied the issues. Dad was a registered

Republican who trusted Mom's judgment. At election time, he simply handed her his sample ballot and asked her how to vote.

I do recall being motivated by President Kennedy's 1961 inaugural address and his historic words: "Ask not what your country can do for you—ask what you can do for your country." I was ten years old at the time.

In high school, we all took the Kuder Career Interests Assessment. The assessment helps people match their interests with potential careers. My interests correlated most highly with public servants/employees and senior pastors. Upon reflection, I do see some similarities between the two professions.

Perhaps, therefore, it is not that surprising that I chose to pursue a career in public service. While completing my bachelor of arts degree in sociology at the University of Southern California, I applied for graduate school programs in public administration, social work, and educational counseling. In fall 1972, I started the master of public administration (MPA) program at USC.

Chapter 2

—*∿*—

THE INTERNSHIP

MANY OF THE USC MPA program classes were conducted at night at the Biltmore Hotel in downtown Los Angeles. This provided convenience for many of the graduate students who had full-time jobs with the federal, state, or city/county governments that had downtown offices. As a twenty-one-year-old student, I felt like I was the only one in my classes who didn't have any government work experience.

During my four years of undergraduate study, I had worked summers and weekends at Marineland of the Pacific. Marineland was an educational oceanarium and entertainment venue on the Palos Verdes Peninsula in the South Bay area of Los Angeles County. I worked in the gift shops trucking inventory from the warehouse, stocking shelves, and ringing up sales at the cash register.

One of my coworkers was Jeannie Martin. One day I was complaining to Jeannie about my first-semester MPA courses and my lack of government work experience. I told her that I felt awkward being in a sea of mid-career professionals who could directly relate the coursework to their jobs. Jeannie responded that her father was the city manager of Manhattan Beach (a South Bay city) and that he regularly employed two graduate students as part-time interns in the city manager's office. She said he already had one intern for the academic year but still wanted to hire another.

That sounded great, I thought, but I had to ask Jeannie an important question: "What's a city manager?" I had never heard of the position or profession. Jeannie replied rather matter-of-factly, "Oh, most people think that the mayor runs a city, but it's really the city manager. Let me call my dad and see if he'll give you an interview."

After a telephone conversation and a personal interview, I gave Marineland my two-weeks' notice and went to work for Manhattan Beach City Manager Gayle T. Martin as a part-time administrative intern.

That was the start of a forty-year career in California city management.

Chapter 3

BEST STAFF REPORT
AND ANALYSIS EVER ... BUT

As THE NEW administrative intern in the Manhattan Beach City Manager's Office, I was given a significant assignment. The city had a private contract for the collection and disposal of all residential and commercial refuse in town. The contractor, Manhattan Beach Disposal, had enjoyed the exclusive contract for many years. The city council requested a comprehensive study and analysis of public versus private refuse collection systems and a staff recommendation on the best option for the future.

I was teamed with Jim, a senior civil engineer from the public works department, to conduct the research and analysis. Jim and I prepared our research outline which included a comprehensive review of private refuse collection contracts in other South Bay cities, as well as refuse collection fee comparisons of municipal and contracted operations. I also wanted to visit some local municipal operations and interview their refuse collection superintendents to get their perspectives on the pros and cons of public versus private service.

One of my first calls was to the owner of Manhattan Beach Disposal. I formally introduced myself as Tim Casey, administrative intern in the Manhattan Beach City Manager's Office. I explained that Jim and I were looking at future options for the provision of refuse collection services in the city and that I wanted to know more about how the company determined its fees for residential and commercial customers in Manhattan Beach. After a long pause, he replied rather loudly, "I don't know who in the hell Tim Casey is, but Gayle Martin is going to hear from me." There was also some reference to cement shoes and the bottom of the Manhattan Beach pier. (No, I'm not kidding.)

City Manager Martin approached my desk and asked, "Did you call the owner of Manhattan Beach Disposal and ask about their refuse collection rates?" "Yes I did," I replied. "Well, I just got an earful from him and they're a little sensitive about those things. I'd suggest that you conduct your research without any more input from him." Lesson learned. Over the course of my ensuing career, I discovered that folks could get pretty worked up about refuse collection, towing service, and ambulance contracts.

My next contact was the refuse superintendent for the City of Inglewood, another South Bay city. Inglewood had a municipal refuse collection system that was recognized as very innovative and efficient. At the time, many residential refuse collection operations employed rear-loading trucks and three-man crews, a driver, and two swampers. The driver drove the truck as the two swampers walked behind tossing cans of trash into the rear hopper and replacing them curbside. As an alternative, the City of Inglewood had pioneered the use of automated side-loading trucks that only required a one-man crew, the driver. The trash cans were mechanically lifted from the curb, dumped into the top of the truck, and returned to the curb mechanically. This approach was revolutionizing refuse collection.

After enjoying a ride-along session with one of Inglewood's refuse truck drivers, the superintendent took me aside to offer a few perspectives about municipal refuse collection systems. His first observation was similar to the US Postal Service: Trash must be picked up without fail, every day, come rain or shine. If an unusual number of drivers call in sick, you sometimes must cannibalize the street or parks departments to secure backup personnel. His second observation was equally valuable. He cautioned me about comparing private versus municipal refuse collection rates. In the private sector, rates are set by business owners who must consider the full cost of service, including overhead, as well as a reasonable profit. In the public sector, rates are set by elected officials (politicians) who do not want to offend their customers (constituents) and don't always take all costs into account.

After many months of research, Jim and I concluded that the best course of action was for the City of Manhattan Beach to continue to contract with the private sector for the collection of residential and commercial refuse. There were several reputable refuse collection companies in Southern California that would love to compete for the city's business. Competitive bidding would keep rates down. Multiyear contracts would permit the successful bidder to amortize capital equipment purchases over a reasonable time period, while allowing the city to retest the market every five to seven years.

We wrapped up our final report, and I was designated to present our findings and recommendation to the city council. It was my first public presentation, and I really practiced and prepared for it. After my presentation, one of the veteran council members praised our work and stated that our report was one of the best he had ever received while serving on the city council. Wow! It was difficult to conceal my smile and sense of pride.

As I returned to my seat in the council chambers, the city council began its deliberations. To my complete surprise, after a very short discussion, the city council voted unanimously to reject our staff recommendation and direct us to take appropriate actions to implement a municipal refuse collection system.

I learned my first lesson that sometimes the most thoughtful and objective research and analysis does not yield a recommendation that will win majority support of the city council. It also taught me that professional implementation of a city council decision that deviated from the staff recommendation is an imperative part of a city manager's responsibilities.

P.S. Approximately ten years later, after I had been appointed city manager for the City of Redondo Beach, the Manhattan Beach City Council again considered its refuse collection and disposal options. The municipal refuse collection experience had not gone as well as hoped, and the city council decided to return to the private contract model.

Chapter 4

PLEASE EDIT THIS;
YOU WRITE BETTER THAN I DO

GAYLE MARTIN WAS a veteran city manager. A civil engineer by educational background, he was also a rear admiral in the US Naval Reserve. He was appointed Manhattan Beach City Manager in the 1950s and had held the position for many years.

The 1974 municipal election had resulted in some turnover on the city council and a new majority with fresh energy, perspective, and ideas. One of their first initiatives was to hire a well-known consulting firm to perform an operational assessment of all city departments and make recommendations for improvement.

The consultant report had been completed, and the city council had scheduled a special meeting to hear the consultant's findings and recommendations. City Manager Martin suggested that I might want to attend the meeting as part of my continuing professional education and enrichment.

The mayor gaveled the meeting to order and invited the consultant team to make its presentation. As I recall, there were some thirty-nine recommendations covering many aspects of the city's operations. Hire a full-time planning director…hire a full-time personnel director… assign certain responsibilities to the assistant to the city manager… update purchasing policies and procedures, etc.

The consultant team worked its way through each recommendation as the council and staff quietly listened.

At the end of the presentation, with few if any questions, the mayor asked if there was a motion and second to approve the consulting firm's report and direct staff to implement all of the recommendations. After a motion and second, the mayor was about to call for the vote when City Manager Martin intervened. "Would the city council like to hear my perspective on the consultant's recommendations?" he asked. "I agree with many of them, but do not think that some are appropriate or workable for the city." Without response, the mayor called for the vote, and the new majority approved the motion to implement all of the recommendations.

City Manager Martin was always the first to arrive at the office each morning. He was always at his desk already working when I would arrive at 8:00 a.m. The next day was no exception. Given his status as a rear admiral in the US Naval Reserve, one of our morning rituals was to poke our head in his office door and request permission to come aboard. After doing so, I retreated to my desk across the hall in the city attorney's office.

Not long after that, City Manager Martin walked in and dropped his yellow legal pad on my desk blotter. "Here," he said. "Please edit this; you write better than I do." I looked down at the legal pad and began to read. It was his resignation letter.

As I recall, the Manhattan Beach Municipal Code required that a public hearing be scheduled to consider the resignation of the city manager. Such a hearing was scheduled, and many residents attended to voice their support for Gayle, urge him to rescind the resignation letter, and/or implore the city council to reject the resignation. After hearing from the residents, the city council voted to accept the resignation, and that was it. My boss was gone, and the city public works director was appointed interim city manager.

P.S. Gayle Martin went on to be become the city manager of La Mesa, California, a city in San Diego County. He completed his career there and in retirement served as the range rider (now known as senior advisor) for all of the cities in Orange County, California. In that role, he served as a senior coach/mentor/advisor to all Orange County city managers representing the International City/County Management Association (ICMA) and the League of California Cities. It has now been my pleasure to serve in that role for seven years.

Chapter 5

———∿∿∿———

THE FIRST FULL-TIME JOB

AFTER MY FIRST semester in the USC MPA program, I transferred to the University of California, Los Angeles (UCLA), to continue my graduate studies. I was attracted to UCLA's curriculum, which included some core public administration and policy courses but also encouraged coursework in other related crossover disciplines (i.e., business, law, architecture). The program also required an internship experience and the completion of a comprehensive paper comparing and contrasting that work experience with the academic and theoretical teachings of the classroom.

Mark was a classmate in several of my courses at UCLA. He was a Vietnam War veteran who had returned from service to pursue his master of public administration degree. It was 1973 and I was starting my second year working for the City of Manhattan Beach in my part-time administrative intern position. Mark had secured a similar position in the nearby City of Torrance under a federally sponsored public employment program. Mark and I hit it off immediately and became good friends.

As we were completing our MPA program, it was time for both of us to seek our first full-time jobs. We began to apply for the same entry-level positions in various cities. One opportunity that caught our eye was an administrative assistant position in the city manager's office in the City of Santa Maria, California. Santa Maria is in the central coast area nestled along the 101 Highway between Santa Barbara and San Luis Obispo.

As luck would have it, Mark and I were invited to interview for the administrative assistant position. After receiving our interview times, we had the audacity to contact the city and ask that our interviews be scheduled back-to-back so we could carpool together. The city granted our request.

It's about a five-hour drive from the South Bay area to Santa Maria. We left at 3:00 a.m. in my Volkswagen Beetle to make our respective 8:30 a.m. and 9:00 a.m. interview times. Mark drove the first leg and then fell asleep in the passenger seat when I took over. He awoke between Santa Barbara and Santa Maria, rubbed the sleep out of his eyes, and looked out the window in the early morning dawn. "S—t, Tim! There are cows out here."

Neither one of us was offered the administrative assistant position in the city manager's office. Interestingly, I must have interviewed well and was offered a similar position with the city's redevelopment agency. I had no idea what a redevelopment agency was or how it operated, so I turned down the offer.

Mark and I next competed for an administrative assistant position in the city manager's office in the City of San Dimas, another Southern California city. San Dimas was a contract city that secured its police and fire services from the county as well as contracting out other services. The administrative assistant was something of a jack-of-all-trades position with a variety of responsibilities, including personnel administration. Mark received the job offer and accepted the position. Upon assuming his new duties, he obtained the civil service test file and called to inform me (i.e., rub it in) that he had outscored me on the written exam and oral interview by a fraction of a percent. It was something like 95.6 percent to 95.3 percent.

Despite my disappointment, I was soon offered an administrative assistant position in the city manager's office in the City of San Buenaventura (Ventura), a full-service coastal city in Ventura County. I gave notice to the City of Manhattan Beach and began my new duties in the City of Ventura in September 1974. My salary was $900 per month plus benefits. Now we're talking!

P.S. Mark went on to pursue a successful professional career in human resource/personnel management. My career followed a more general management path always working in the city manager's office. We stayed in touch and finished our careers serving cities in Orange County, California. Mark served for many years as the personnel director for the City of Fullerton while I completed my career serving twenty-two years as the first city manager of the City of Laguna Niguel.

Chapter 6

———⁓⁓———

GETTING TO YES AND ETHICS 101

THE CALL CAME from the code enforcement division downstairs. There were two angry men who had been cited for illegally operating a seasonal Christmas tree sales lot on vacant property in the downtown area. They were demanding to see the city manager. Obviously, that wasn't going to happen, so the next best choice was to have them meet with the new greenhorn administrative assistant in the city manager's office.

I walked downstairs to meet these gentlemen and introduce myself. They were a little rough around the edges but certainly fit my image of Christmas tree salesmen in the 1970s: long hair, unkempt beards, flannel plaid shirts, blue jeans, and hiking boots. I invited them upstairs to my office.

"What's the problem?" I asked. They described how they had hoped to make a few honest bucks selling trees during the holiday season. They had secured a good supply of trees and set up shop in the city. "Why were you cited?" I inquired. "Well, we didn't have a business license," one replied. "That shouldn't be a problem. Seasonal business licenses aren't expensive," I responded. "Well, we also don't own the

15

property and didn't get permission from the property owner," the other offered. "OK, that's a problem," I conceded.

That could have been the end of the discussion, but for some reason I wanted to help out these guys. My tiny apartment was walking distance from the supermarket where I shopped, and I knew there was a large vacant lot next to the store. I contacted the store manager and was informed that the vacant lot was owned by the grocery store company. For a reasonable rent, they would welcome a Christmas tree lot on their site.

A rental agreement was arranged, and my new best friends moved all of their tree inventory and materials to the new site. For the next several weeks, I made my usual trips to the market, always stopping to say hello to them and see how they were doing. By Christmas, there were very few trees left on the lot.

After Christmas, I opened my front door and a beautifully wrapped package fell into my entryway. It was a brand-new fishing rod and reel with a thank-you note from the guys. I wasn't sure how they had found out where I lived. I returned to the market and found them breaking down the lot. I returned the gift and explained why I could not accept it. "I was just doing my job," I told them. With that, I wished them good luck in the future, and they thanked me for my assistance. I assumed I would never see them again.

P.S. Ventura City Hall was a beautifully converted old courthouse at the top of California Street. However, the property provided little off-street parking. I would park each morning in an adjacent residential neighborhood and cross a pedestrian bridge that led to one of the second-floor entrances to the building. Before crossing the bridge, I would pass a series of portable buildings that Ventura County was using as courtrooms.

As I passed the courtrooms one morning, two voices rang out, "Hey, Tim, how are you doing?" As I glanced toward the courtrooms, I saw my two Christmas tree sales friends in orange jumpsuits, handcuffed and shackled at the ankles. "What happened?" I asked. The good news was that my friends had a highly successful Christmas sales season. The bad news is that they drank their profits (literally), got into a scuffle with locals outside a downtown bar, and got arrested.

That was the last time I ever saw them.

Chapter 7

The Pool in the Park

After turning the Christmas tree lot problem into a solution, another interesting challenge came my way. The City of Ventura had several parks that abutted residential neighborhoods. The parks were not fenced, so the property line between parkland and homeowner's land was not easily determined without an engineering survey.

One day, I was called into a meeting with other staff from the city manager's office, parks department, and engineering division. It appeared that a resident had built a new swimming pool in his backyard, or at least what he thought was his backyard. An engineering survey confirmed that the pool was in the adjacent city park. The options were limited: order the demolition and removal of the new pool or find a way to sell the park property to the adjacent homeowner.

The pool and deck area were small, so the encroachment onto the park property was minimal. City staff collectively decided to find a way to sell the property to the homeowner. However, state law didn't allow the city to simply negotiate a fair price and sell the property.

The first step was to prepare a metes and bounds legal description of the encroachment area. Then, the city council had to formally declare the described property surplus to the city's parks and recreation needs. Finally, the city council had to set a minimum bid price, advertise the property for sale, and accept the highest bid.

As I recall, the city placed the bid advertisement in one of the local general-circulation newspapers in the most inconspicuous location for the minimally required advertising time. As the bid deadline approached, I found myself losing some sleep. What if someone saw the ad, thought it would be fun to own a pool in the park, and outbid the adjacent homeowner?

Fortunately, my worst fears were never realized. At bid opening, there was only one bid. The careless property owner kept his pool, the loss of park space was negligible, and the city made a few dollars.

Chapter 8

———∿∿∿———

TWENTY-FOUR-HOUR NOTICE

THE JOB OFFER from the City of Ventura had seemed perfect. Aside from the refuse collection study, the internship with the City of Manhattan Beach had several duties and responsibilities that were typical of many internships: ghost writing, complaint handling, press releases, newsletter articles. The Ventura position offered some new and exciting responsibilities, such as budget analysis, operations research, and being part of the labor negotiations team.

Things started well at first, but a few months into the job things changed. The city council had concluded that the organization needed to place greater emphasis on public information and communications. The city did not have a public information officer, and there was little interest in creating a new full-time position. With two administrative assistants in the city manager's office, it was clear that one of us was going to be redirected to assume these new duties. My coworker Miriam was senior to me and had a strong background in economics and finance. My administrative intern duties in Manhattan Beach had included many of the things that the city council wanted to prioritize. The choice was clear.

I took on the responsibility for creating a more robust public information program. I was able to hire and supervise a citizen services assistant who was stationed at a desk near the first-floor entrance to the city hall and was the first face and voice of the city to personally greet and assist the public. She was great, but I grew increasingly frustrated with the new responsibilities and lack of professional growth.

About nine months into the position, I was disenchanted and started to wonder if I had made the right career choice. On a Thursday afternoon, I marched into the city manager's office and made one of the most impulsive decisions of my short lifetime. "Ed, I'm quitting," I boldly stated. City Manager Ed McCombs quietly asked me why, and I explained my frustrations. "So, are you giving two weeks' notice?" he calmly asked. "No," I replied. "I'm leaving tomorrow." He responded, "OK, why don't we get together tomorrow afternoon at Jack's at the Beach. We can have a couple of beers and give you a proper farewell."

Ed and I met at Jack's at the Beach around three o'clock on Friday afternoon. We shared a few beers and a few laughs and reflected on my nine months with the city. As we parted company, Ed put his hand on my shoulder and said, "You'll be back."

P.S. First, I do not recommend that anyone ever walk out of a job without giving proper written notice. My impulsive departure was immature, embarrassing, and the most unprofessional action of my career. However, City Manager McCombs's handling of the situation was gracious, supportive, and reassuring. Fifteen years later, I would be starting my second city manager position as the first city manager of the newly incorporated City of Laguna Niguel in Orange County, California. The first congratulatory card came from Ed, whom I had occasionally encountered during the intervening years. In the card, Ed wrote, "I've been admiring your career from afar. I told you that you'd be back."

Chapter 9

———— ∼∼∼ ————

A QUICK BOUNCE BACK

AFTER MY DEPARTURE from the City of Ventura, I returned home to the South Bay and sought employment again with Marineland of the Pacific. One of my former coworkers, Craig Mitchell, had been named director of guest relations. I reached out to him, and he managed to convince Marineland management that he could use an assistant. I soon found myself back at the oceanarium as the new assistant director of guest relations.

Bob Riley was the new young city manager for the City of Redondo Beach. Bob had been the director of administrative services for Redondo Beach while I was doing my internship with the City of Manhattan Beach. In the 1970s, the South Bay Cities had begun conducting an annual total compensation survey for certain benchmark classifications to assist all cities in the labor negotiations process. I had volunteered to lead the data collection effort, which required me to drive to each South Bay city, meet with each personnel director (or other responsible manager), and gather salary and benefit data for each benchmark position. It was a manual tabulation exercise that resulted in a *Total Compensation Survey* booklet, which was compiled and printed for each city.

As the director of administrative services, Bob was my point of contact for the City of Redondo Beach. I scheduled an appointment with Bob, met with him, and gathered the information that I needed for the survey. Apparently, he saw some promise in my city management future. About the time I was heading to the City of Ventura, Bob was appointed city manager in Redondo Beach. At the time, he was one of the youngest city managers in California, about twenty-seven years old as I recall. Sometime after my arrival in Ventura, Bob called to offer me a position as an entry-level analyst in his office. I respectfully declined the offer since I had only been in Ventura for a few months.

Apparently, word of my return to the South Bay reached Bob shortly after I returned to Marineland. He tracked me down and informed me that he had never filled the budgeted analyst position. It was still mine if I was interested. I told Bob that the experience in Ventura had somewhat soured my city management career aspirations and that I wasn't sure I was ready to give it another try. Bob suggested that I attend a Redondo Beach City Council meeting to observe the council/staff/community interaction and reconsider the job offer after that. I politely promised to do so.

The Redondo Beach City Council met weekly on Monday nights. As I drove into the parking lot a week or two later, I still wondered if I really wanted another position in local government or if I was only doing this as a courtesy to Bob. I entered the council chambers and sat in the far back corner.

During the 1960s and 1970s, the City of Redondo Beach had rezoned its coastal waterfront to permit higher-density multifamily residential development. Multistory apartment buildings had replaced single-family homes. Additionally, the harbor/pier area had been redeveloped with several boat marinas and waterside restaurants, retail shops and apartments. The land use changes and increased density had not settled well with many old-time residents.

The city council agenda included a public comment period when anyone could address the council on any item of municipal concern.

From my seat in the corner, I watched numerous residents stride to the microphone and decry the development and redevelopment activity taking place in the city's coastal area. Most ended their comments by asking for Bob's resignation or termination. That was enough for me. I exited the meeting determined to return to Marineland and my new position. Maybe I could work toward a promotion as a killer whale or dolphin trainer.

A few weeks later, Bob called again. "Hey," he said, "I saw you in the audience at the council meeting a few weeks ago. What did you think?" "It looks to me like the whole town wants your head on a platter," I replied. "Aw, those are just the local gadflies. They criticize everything we do. Their bark is worse than their bite. I still want you to come and work for me," he concluded.

Two weeks later, I started my new position as analyst in the city manager's office of the City of Redondo Beach.

Chapter 10

They're Not All Rocket Scientists

ALTHOUGH I WASN'T part of the executive team, Bob encouraged me to attend city council meetings to stay informed of current issues. There were enough seats in the staff section of the council chambers to give me a close-up view of the proceedings.

There were three boat basins in the Redondo Beach Marina. Basin 3 was the southernmost section surrounded on four sides by a concrete quay wall and a small channel entrance to the docks that served commercial fishing boats, private boats, and a commercially operated public boat launching hoist. An asphalt public boardwalk had been developed atop the quay wall, which also hosted numerous restaurants, take-out food establishments, a fresh seafood store, souvenir stores, and an amusement/game parlor. The multicultural nature of the cuisine had led to the area being dubbed the International Boardwalk.

Winter storms often caused damage to the Redondo Beach harbor and pier area. A combination of high tides and storm surge had undermined and damaged a portion of the International Boardwalk quay wall. Step one of the proposed engineering solution was to bring in tons of Catalina rock by barge and carefully place the rock by crane in the water at the base of the failed quay wall to bolster its foundation. Step two was to pressure-fill the surface fissures of the quay wall with a slurry cement-mud grout to fill the subsurface voids.

As I watched the city engineer make his presentation to the city council, I couldn't help but notice concern on the face of the District 2 councilman. Redondo Beach was a charter city with a directly elected mayor and a five-member city council elected by district. The District 2 councilmember represented the harbor and pier area.

As the city engineer explained the proposal to place the Catalina rock in Basin 3, the District 2 councilman was playing with the ice in his water glass. He was using his pencil to push the ice cubes down into the glass. The downward pressure on the ice would displace the water and cause it to rise to the rim of the glass.

After the city engineer completed his presentation, the mayor called for any city council questions. The District 2 councilman asked to be recognized and turned on his microphone. He complimented the city engineer and raised his concern. Plunging his pencil again into his water glass to punctuate the point, he asked the city engineer, "If we dump these tons and tons of Catalina rock into Basin 3, don't we run the risk of overtopping the basin and flooding the adjacent businesses?" Without missing a beat, the city engineer calmly replied, "Councilman, I understand and appreciate the physical phenomenon that you are demonstrating, but you have to remember one thing: the Pacific Ocean is one big glass of water."

Case closed.

Chapter 11

FREEDOM OF SPEECH AND FREEDOM OF THE PRESS

THE MAYOR HAD been particularly upset by the proliferation of adult newsstands on the streets and sidewalks of the city. The city attorney had advised that the city could regulate the number, size, and placement of the news racks to promote pedestrian safety but could not ban the racks or the adult content of the material.

One night, I observed the mayor enter the council chambers with numerous newspapers folded under his arm. The look on his face made it clear that he was not a happy camper.

As the meeting began, the mayor invited public comments of a general nature on subjects not appearing on the agenda. A resident who regularly attended city council meetings approached the podium and began her weekly assault on the mayor and city council. As she worked her way through her three minutes of criticism, the mayor was becoming visibly agitated.

Before she could complete her remarks, the mayor interrupted. "Ma'am," he started, "there are abuses of the freedom of speech just as there are abuses of the freedom of the press." Then he reached into his pile of newspapers, found the one he was looking for, and thrust the cover page over the dais as far toward the public podium as he could reach. My sense of decency and decorum prevents me from graphically describing the photo on the cover page of the adult newspaper. Suffice it to say, it would meet any reasonable person's definition of pornography.

The resident speaker was clearly mortified by the image and the mayor's behavior. She retreated from the podium and returned to her seat.

A claim and lawsuit followed. As I recall, the lawsuit was dismissed in light of the free speech protections granted to public officials. However, the city (or its insurance company) did incur some cost to defend the mayor's conduct.

Chapter 12

~~~

DOES THIS QUALIFY?

THE US SUPREME Court had made it clear. A municipality may place reasonable restrictions on the location of adult business establishments (i.e., adult bookstores, theaters, strip clubs) but could not ban them completely from the community. As a result, it would be necessary to amend the city's zoning ordinance to comply with the court's decision.

The city's planning department staff initiated the drafting of an ordinance that would satisfy the reasonable time, manner, and place standards that the court had found acceptable in Young v. American Mini Theatres (1976). The challenge was to identify areas of the city where adult business establishments would be permitted.

The court had endorsed reasonable space separation regulations. For example, it appeared permissible for a city to restrict the operation of adult businesses within a reasonable distance from schools and from other adult business uses. In the Young case, the court had found that a one-thousand-foot separation between adult businesses was reasonable to avoid a concentration of such businesses and their secondary effects on the community.

After considering the options, it was determined that the imposition of reasonable space separation regulations would leave two areas of the city open to adult businesses: the northeast corner of the city and the southwest corner of the city. The permissible area in the southwest fell within Riviera Village, an upscale collection of restaurants, offices, retail shops, and clothing boutiques. While Riviera Village consisted of multiple landlords and property owners, its upscale stature suggested that the property owners/landlords would probably not lease to an adult business.

One Riviera Village store owner was not convinced. Fred had owned and operated Catalina Book and Music for many years. It was an independent book and music store with a wonderful, eclectic selection of books and records. The last thing that Fred wanted to see was the opening of an adult business in the village.

As I walked into the council chambers for the weekly council meeting, I saw Fred sitting in the audience. During the opportunity for public comment, Fred picked up a large, heavy cardboard box and strode to the microphone. He addressed the council and expressed his concerns about the possibility of an adult business setting up shop in Riviera Village. Then he informed the council that he would like the city to designate Catalina Book and Music as an adult business establishment.

To validate his request, Fred opened the cardboard box and began to remove books. They were largely photography books, the type that you might place on the coffee table in your living room. As he continued to speak, Fred deftly turned to the earmarked pages of several books and held them up for the councilmembers and audience to see. "Does this qualify?" he would ask as he moved from page to page and book to book.

The earmarked pages were all photographs of nude men and/or women in various poses. In many respects, the pictures were beautiful and tasteful as one might expect in a professional book of photography. Fred's objective, however, was to have the council declare the books obscene. Soon the books and pictures were circulating from councilmember to councilmember to city staff.

To the best of my recollection, the city council conceded that the collection of photography books with naked human images qualified Catalina Book and Music as an adult business. Given the location of the store, there was no other location within the Riviera Village area that could accommodate another adult business. Fred had gotten his way.

Chapter 13

———∽∿∽———

A SECOND DATE?

AS ASSISTANT TO the city manager, I was responsible for directing the work of and supervising the administrative intern in our office. Bob was older than me and had been working as a full-time ride supervisor at Disneyland in Anaheim, California. He had just completed his master's degree in political science at UC Santa Barbara. He was looking for his first job in local government, and we hired him as a part-time administrative intern.

Bob lived in an apartment complex called Pathways near Cal State Long Beach. It was a sprawling complex with multiple swimming pools, sand volleyball courts, and a largely young and single group of tenants. Bob was single and I was single, and we became friends quickly.

On a few occasions, Bob had mentioned that he had a cute neighbor down the hall from his apartment at Pathways. He thought that she and I might hit it off, but he was reluctant to set up a blind date because she would consent to joining him for dinner or a movie if neither had something better lined up on a Friday night. It was a purely platonic relationship.

Sometime before Christmas 1977, Bob decided it was time for me to meet Rosalind Rice. He was having a Christmas party and invited me to get a date (preferably someone that I was not interested in) and come to the party. He would also invite Rosalind and find a way to introduce us during the event. I agreed.

The Redondo Beach City Manager's sister-in-law, who was about my age, was visiting for the holidays, and he had asked if I would invite her out while she was in town. I invited her to the Christmas party, explained the game plan, and she agreed to go. We arrived at Bob's apartment and enjoyed the party, but Rosalind was a no-show.

Undaunted by the failed connection, but determined to succeed, Bob contacted Rosalind and explained the plan that he had concocted. He asked if he could give me Rosalind's phone number. She was reluctant but ultimately agreed after Bob told her that she had met me in the Pathways parking lot on a prior occasion. That was a complete lie.

I think that I placed that first call to Rosalind within five minutes of receiving her number. We laughed a little bit about Bob's failed plan to introduce us to each other. I told her that a couple had invited me to attend the Rose Bowl game with them and if she would consider going on a double date. She was hesitant to say yes. She had just ended a relationship and was not ready to start another one. I was persistent that it would be a fun day, and she finally consented. To be honest, given my gift for gab, I think she said yes out of clear exhaustion to get me off the phone.

The 1978 Rose Bowl was scheduled for Monday, January 2, rather than the usual New Year's Day date. The 64th Rose Bowl game matched up the Washington Huskies, winners of the Pacific 8 Conference, and the Michigan Wolverines, winners of the Big Ten Conference.

I arrived at Pathways in my green Toyota Corolla and found my way to Rosalind's apartment. I rang the doorbell, the door opened, and there was Rosalind. When she saw me, I am sure her first thought was "I've never met this guy before." We both had vivid first impressions. Roz was very tall, had her hair up in a bun, and was wearing excessive blue eye makeup. I was wearing a turtleneck sweater and earth shoes, which I later learned were Roz's two most-hated items of men's apparel. It was a match made in heaven. We drove back to Torrance, California, to join my friends and carpool to the Rose Bowl. A little hot buttered rum in the back seat helped take the edge off things.

The game looked like it was going to be a blowout. The Huskies led by 17–0 at halftime and added another touchdown in the third quarter to make it 24–0. During the fan celebration following that score, Roz leaned over and gave me a sweet kiss on the cheek. "Oh my gosh," I thought. "She doesn't think I'm a turkey."

It turned out to be a great day and a great first date, and I was eager to ask Roz out again. I called and asked if I could see her later that week. I also had decided that if our dating was going to continue, Roz needed to know more about my job and the city management profession.

I pulled into the Pathways parking lot in the evening, greeted Roz, and handed her a paper bag. It was filled with past issues of *Public Management* (the monthly publication of the International City/County Management Association) and *Western City* magazine (the monthly publication of the League of California Cities). "Read these," I told her. "This is what I do. After you're done, let me know if you'd like to go on a second date."

Roz and I celebrated our fortieth wedding anniversary on September 22, 2019.

Chapter 14

❧

PROPOSITION 13—
NO LAYOFF BUT A PROMOTION?

IN JUNE 1978, California voters approved Proposition 13, the infamous property-tax slashing ballot initiative. Overnight, California's local governments (i.e., counties, cities, and special districts) saw two-thirds of their property tax revenue disappear.

Redondo Beach, like most California cities, had prepared two budgets for FY 78–79—one with a green cover if Proposition 13 failed and one with a red cover if Proposition 13 passed. At the time, I was one of two administrative assistants in the city manager's office, having been promoted from my original analyst position. My duties and responsibilities were general in nature while Roger, the other administrative assistant, was more focused on budget and finance. The city manager felt the need to demonstrate that if Proposition 13 was approved, his office would not be immune from the necessary cutbacks and layoffs. As a result, the red budget called for the elimination of one of the administrative assistant positions.

When I awoke on the morning after Election Day and saw the

Proposition 13 results, I assumed my position was doomed. The city manager's office really needed a budget and finance specialist since, by charter, the elected city clerk was the city's finance officer (with minimal education requirements and no experience necessary). After three years of employment with the city, Marineland was looking surprisingly good again.

As a full-service city with over six hundred full-time employees, Redondo Beach had a fully staffed personnel department. The personnel director had been recently recruited from the private sector and was acclimating herself to the structure and inflexibility of public sector personnel and civil service systems (i.e., written tests and exams, employment eligibility lists, the Rule of One or the Rule of Three hiring restrictions, long probation periods, etc.). Unbeknownst to me, she was yearning to return to the private sector.

The personnel director approached the city manager with a proposition: I am not happy and am going to resign to pursue new opportunities. Tim has been involved in personnel issues and labor negotiations; I think he can oversee and manage the personnel department.

Rather than lose my job, I got a promotion…without a new title or additional compensation, of course.

Chapter 15

THE PERVERSE INCENTIVE

SHORTLY AFTER PROPOSITION 13, City Manager Riley announced his resignation to accept an executive position with a Southern California-based general contracting firm. The firm's owner had been impressed with Bob's involvement in siting and permitting a major beverage distribution facility in North Redondo. The city conducted an executive search and hired Dave Dolter, the assistant city manager in Santa Monica, as the new Redondo Beach city manager.

As I recall, Dave assumed his new duties in December 1978. At the time, Redondo Beach did not have an assistant city manager. There was a director of administrative services who often served as acting city manager in the boss's absence. Additionally, there were the two administrative assistant positions: my position (now focused on personnel management, city council agenda coordination, and special projects) and Roger's position still focused on budget and finance. Shortly after his hiring, Dave reclassified the two administrative assistant positions; Roger and I were now officially assistants to the city manager. There was a compensation increase this time.

The director of administrative services had accepted a similar position with the City of Walnut Creek and departed to Northern California. Sometime afterward, Dave approached Roger and me with a most unusual proposition. He declared that as soon of one of us left Redondo Beach for a new position elsewhere, he would take action to promote and name the other one assistant city manager. I found that to be a very interesting and perverse promotional incentive.

Roger and I both had been pursuing other professional opportunities. Roger was still interested in positions that would keep him involved in budget and finance. I was starting to look at city manager opportunities and had already cracked my first interview with the City of San Luis Obispo (see next chapter).

Roger got the first offer to become the new director of administrative services for the City of Culver City, another South Bay community. He accepted the job. True to his word, City Manager Dolter called me into his office and said he was ready to name me assistant city manager, the clear No. 2 spot on the city's executive team.

I thanked Dave for the offer but explained that I had a predicament. I had been interviewing for the position of city manager with the City of Palos Verdes Estates (my hometown) and had been informed that I was a strong finalist. This was around May or June 1980. However, the Palos Verdes Estates City Council had thrown a small wrench into the selection process. A majority of the city council declared that they would not be seeking reelection in November and that the new city council should have the opportunity to appoint the next city manager.

Dave was pretty blunt. "I can't wait that long to see if you get the position. A bird in the hand is better than two in the bush. Make a decision."

In July 1980, I was appointed assistant city manager for the City of Redondo Beach. Less than a year later, that turned out to be an excellent decision.

Chapter 16

———∿∿———

THE FIRST CITY MANAGER INTERVIEW

SEVEN YEARS IN the business seemed long enough. The recruitment brochure from the City of San Luis Obispo looked interesting. Located in the California Central Coast, the full-service city was recruiting a new city manager. The city had a good reputation, was the home to a state university campus and a beautiful downtown, and had a strong agricultural base. As a freshly minted assistant to the city manager, I figured nothing ventured, nothing gained. I submitted my cover letter and résumé and, to my pleasant surprise, was invited for an interview.

The flight from Los Angeles International Airport to the San Luis Obispo Regional Airport was a rocky one. It was a nine-seat plane, and the weather was terrible, so it was a stormy, turbulence-filled ride. We arrived safely, and I grabbed a taxi for the ride to the downtown hotel where interviews were being conducted.

The councilmembers were warm and friendly. After the obligatory self-introduction and summary of my background, the specific questions began.

What experience do you have in a developing community? None.

What experience do you have in a college town? None.

What experience do you have with growth control ordinances? None.

What experience do you have working with an agricultural community and the Williamson Act? None.

Suddenly the questions ceased. We were only about ten minutes into the allotted one-hour interview. After a long pause, I spoke. "If I leave right now, I think I can catch the eleven a.m. flight back to LA." Everyone agreed that would be a good idea.

P.S. Sometimes rejection is a good thing. In retrospect, this would not have been a good professional fit. At least I got a unanimous vote.

Chapter 17

~~~

LOOK RIGHT, LOOK LEFT...
AND LOOK BACK

As ASSISTANT TO the city manager and as assistant city manager, one of my responsibilities was risk management and insurance administration. The City of Redondo Beach had two fire stations, Fire Station No. 1 in South Redondo and Fire Station No. 2 in North Redondo. Fire Station No. 1 was located at 401 South Broadway at its intersection with Pearl Street.

One day, I was summoned from city hall to Fire Station No. 1 to document a traffic accident involving the hook and ladder truck assigned to the station. The truck was the type in which a fire engineer drove from the front cab and a tillerman steered the ladder trailer section from the back. The cab and the ladder trailer were connected by a hinge mechanism to facilitate turning movements.

When I arrived on the scene, there was a carnage of damaged cars on Pearl Street and the back of the ladder truck was heavily damaged. Fortunately, there were no injuries.

As I interviewed the personnel assigned to the truck, the details of the accident quickly became clear. A call was dispatched to Fire Station No. 1 requiring a response from the hook and ladder truck and crew. The crew quickly donned their turnout gear and raced to their positions on the truck. The fire engineer/driver took his seat in the cab, and the supporting firefighters took their positions on the running boards. After a look to the left and a look to the right for any oncoming traffic, the fire engineer/driver pulled out of the station onto South Broadway for the Code 3 response.

The exit/turn onto South Broadway went smoothly, but the next quick left turn onto Pearl Street did not. The ladder section of the truck jackknifed to the right and began sideswiping one parked car after another. A look back by the fire engineer/driver resulted in a shocking discovery: where was the tillerman? As it turned out, he never made it onto the truck. Let's just say he was indisposed on the commode in the fire station.

As I recall, the city (and our liability insurance company) bought a few used cars that day. Needless to say, the incident led to some changes in fire department policies and procedures.

Chapter 18

AN APOLOGY...
FROM THE POLICE CHIEF?

My PERSONNEL MANAGEMENT responsibilities required that I approve all new hires. The city had embarked on an aggressive recruitment campaign to hire trained and experienced police officers from other agencies through lateral transfer. That required regular collaboration with the police chief.

One application file that landed on my desk gave me pause. The applicant was a police officer from a neighboring South Bay city. He had the requisite experience, but there were some troubling aspects to his file. It appeared that he had filed several workers' compensation injury claims and had a series of traffic accidents with his current employer. I told the police chief that I would not approve the hiring.

At that stage of my career, it had been my personal observation (right or wrong) that many police chiefs didn't like to be told that they couldn't do something—not by the city manager, but especially by a twenty-nine-year-old flash-in-the-pan assistant. The police chief appealed my decision to the city manager. We met in the city manager's office and presented our respective arguments for and against the hiring of the applicant. The police chief won. I lost.

It wasn't long after the new hire started work that he was dispatched to respond to a loud and boisterous party call in North Redondo. Arriving on scene, he encountered a large party of forty to fifty people that had spilled onto the public streets. Before backups arrived, he tried to disperse the crowd and coax the people back into the home where the party had begun.

Not surprisingly, one partygoer became very loud and belligerent, thereby flunking the attitude test. He was placed under arrest, handcuffed, and put in the back of the patrol car. The police officer resumed his attempts at crowd control. The arrestee, however, was not done. He began screaming and kicking at the safety screen and windows of the patrol car. At that point, the police officer removed the arrestee from the back seat of the car, opened his trunk, threw him in, and closed the lid...in front of forty to fifty witnesses.

The newly hired lateral transfer did not see the end of his probationary period. After his termination, the police chief invited me to lunch and offered a sincere apology. I had been right. He had been wrong. We ended the afternoon with a few too many drinks at the Blue Moon Saloon and didn't make it back to work that day.

Chapter 19

AND OTHER DUTIES AS REQUIRED

AS ASSISTANT CITY manager, it was my responsibility to serve as acting city manager when the boss was on vacation or traveling on city business. That occurred several times after my appointment, but one occasion was most memorable.

The city manager and a councilmember had traveled to Sacramento, the state capital, on city business. Around 9:00 p.m., the phone rang. It was the watch commander from the police department.

"Tim," he said, "we have a little problem here and could use your assistance." "What's going on?" I asked. As it turned out, the traveling councilmember's wife had enjoyed a few too many adult beverages that evening and had been pulled over for drunk driving. Upon identifying and recognizing who he had pulled over, the police officer transported her to the police station where she was placed in the drunk tank, a jail cell with padded walls for the safety of the occupants.

"What do you want me to do about it?" I asked. "Well, we thought maybe you could come by, pick her up, and take her back to your house until she sobers up," he thoughtfully suggested. I explained the situation to my wife, who quickly exclaimed, "She's not coming here!" Smart woman.

I knew that the councilmember's wife had some close friends in the community, so I pulled out the telephone book and started looking for names and numbers. After a few calls, I connected with a friend who agreed to take her in if I would drive her to the house. I called the watch commander to inform him that I was on my way for the pickup and transfer. He advised me to pull into the secure parking lot behind the police station where someone would be stationed to allow my entry.

It was about 11:00 p.m. when I pulled into the back parking area of the station and stopped my car by a back entry door. The door slowly opened, and two police personnel awkwardly helped a blanket-covered person into the front passenger seat of my car. As I pulled away from the station, my groggy passenger pulled the blanket from her head and had a good look at me. "Hey, I know who you are," she slurred. "You're that fire captain, Tom King." Without hesitation, I replied, "Yes I am, Mrs. Smith. Yes I am."

Chapter 20

ONE WEEK'S NOTICE

IT WAS MAY 1981 and Roz and I were expecting our first child. The due date was May 9. I had informed City Manager Dolter that when the baby arrived, I intended to take off a week to support Roz and our newborn. Dave totally understood even though we were in the midst of labor negotiations (I was the city's chief negotiator) and the FY 81– 82 Proposed City Budget was due to the city council by mid-May.

Better late than never, Shannon Marisa Casey was born at 3:32 p.m. on Sunday, May 17. I called Dave to inform him that I was a proud new dad and that I wouldn't be in to work on Monday or any-time that week. Dave extended his congratulations to Roz and me.

Back then, the Redondo Beach City Council met weekly on Monday nights. I wasn't expecting any late-night phone calls that eve-ning, but on Monday, May 18, the phone rang at about 11:00 p.m. I answered and it was Dave.

"How are Roz and Shannon doing?" he asked. "They're doing great," I replied. "How are you doing?" he continued. "I'm doing fine," I responded. "Why are you calling?" The response was not what I ex-pected to hear at that moment. "I quit tonight," Dave bluntly reported.

I knew that Dave had not been happy with the job. The directly elected mayor had a strong and dominant personality and tended to run roughshod over the city council and city staff. The council members, in turn, expected the city manager to be a strong offensive and defensive buffer between them and the mayor. Even though a new mayor had just been elected, Dave was worn out. He had been looking for other opportunities in the public and private sectors.

I asked Dave, "So what did you do? Give them thirty days' notice?" "Nope," Dave replied, "I'm clearing out my office by Friday. When you get back next Monday, you'll be the acting city manager."

And that was that. When I returned to city hall on Monday, May 25, Dave was gone and the city manager's office was largely vacant, but for his empty desk and credenza, a few working files that Dave had left for me, and the notebook containing that night's city council agenda. I had already communicated with the new mayor and spent the rest of the day moving my office files and personal belongings into the office and preparing for the council meeting.

Later that evening, the city council ratified my appointment as acting city manager, directed me to seek proposals from executive search firms for a national recruitment for the next city manager, and encouraged me to apply for the job.

Chapter 21

KIDNEY STONES AND LABOR PAINS

IT HAD BEEN quite a month. On April 29, 1981, my mother died after a long bout with cancer. She missed the birth of her only grandchild by less than three weeks. On May 17, our daughter Shannon was born. On May 18, the Redondo Beach city manager resigned, and on May 25, I assumed my duties as acting city manager.

There is a list of life events that can be real stressors. The list includes death of a family member, birth of a child, and a significant job change. I had experienced all of them in a very short time period. All that was missing was a serious illness or injury.

After the arrival of our daughter, Roz and I were looking forward to a date night. My father agreed to babysit, and we invited a friend and his girlfriend to join us for dinner at the Blue Moon Saloon in Redondo Beach's King Harbor. When we were seated at our restaurant table, we decided to celebrate. We ordered exotic cocktails and lobster tails with melted butter and all the side dishes.

From the moment we sat down, I just couldn't get comfortable in my seat. I felt very nauseous, and there was a sharp pain growing in my back. I thought it was probably just gas, so I excused myself and went to the men's room. Without much success, I returned to the table and sat down. As dinner was served, I knew I was in trouble. We left the lobster on the table, and I asked Roz to drive me home. We didn't make it that far.

As we approached the street that I knew led to South Bay Hospital, I told Roz that we better detour to the emergency room. We arrived a few minutes later and parked, and Roz helped me painfully make my way to the admissions lobby. I sat down on a bench while Roz approached the admissions clerk to explain my situation. It was a Saturday night and the ER was filled with other patients waiting to be treated. Before I knew it, I was being taken to an examination room ahead of the others.

After blood and urine tests and some imaging, the diagnosis was made: I had a pretty good-sized kidney stone in the shape of an arrowhead that had punctured my ureter and was leaking uric acid into my system. I was not going home that night. It would be the first and only hospitalization of my life (to date).

In the wee hours of Sunday morning, I was rolled to my room in a wheelchair by a helpful attendant. Still groggy from the painkiller, I heard a voice whisper in my ear, "Don't worry, Mr. Casey. You're in good hands. I'm a Redondo Beach police officer." Looking around, I saw the vaguely familiar face of an officer named Paul. He informed me that he had been a medic during his service in the Vietnam War and moonlighted at the hospital to make a few extra dollars. A few seconds later, he leaned over and spoke again. "Mr. Casey, I hate to take advantage of a captive patient, but it really is a shame that Hermosa Beach cops make more than we do." It reminded me that we were in the midst of negotiations with the Redondo Beach Police Association and that being a city manager (even an acting city manager) is a 24/7 job.

My stay in the hospital lasted three days, but this first episode was not the end of my "labor" pains. I shared a hospital room with another patient, and my bed was the closest to the window. On Monday night about 11:00 p.m., I was about to get some sleep when I noticed the door to the hallway open. Three to four shadowy, giggling figures quietly sneaked in. Soon I felt my bed (and IV solution) being rolled toward the window. A familiar voice teasingly threatened, "Tim, it's time to settle our contract or you're going out the window." It was the police negotiating team.

Chapter 22

I Get the Job … on a 3–2 Vote

After City Manager Dolter's abrupt departure, the Redondo Beach City Council confirmed my appointment as acting city manager on May 25, 1981. At the same meeting, the council directed me to seek proposals from executive search firms to conduct a nationwide recruitment for the next city manager, and they encouraged me to apply. I was thirty years old.

I was determined to make the most of this opportunity. From my perspective, I was in an enviable risk-free position. If I worked my tail off for the next four to six months and convinced them that I was fully capable of running the city, perhaps they would offer me the permanent position. If that did not happen, I would simply resume my duties and responsibilities as assistant city manager (a position that I had not yet held for one year) and do my best to support the next city manager.

Things went well during the next six months. The city council approved the FY 81–82 City Budget, and labor agreements were reached with the police association and other bargaining units. Progress was being made on the city's work program and capital improvement plan.

After several interviews with prospective city manager candidates, I was informed that I was in the final two for the job.

As the city council met in its final closed session before publicly announcing and voting on the city manager appointment, I impatiently waited for the council to reconvene in open session. The hints and whispers were that I was going to be offered the job. I had heard that the other finalist was a veteran city manager from another Southern California city who had attended Redondo Union High School and was the preferred candidate of one councilmember. I was expecting to be appointed by a 4–1 vote.

As the city council entered the council chambers, a few winks and nods reinforced my confidence. After the council was seated, the mayor asked if anyone would like to offer a motion. For the life of me, I can't remember who made the motion or offered the second, but the motion was put on the table to appoint Timothy J. Casey as the next city manager of the City of Redondo Beach. After minimal discussion, the mayor called for the vote, which was done by machine with green and red lights denoting yes and no votes. The lights appeared on the wall-mounted voting board next to the names of each councilmember.

When I looked up, there were three green lights and two red lights. What? One red light appeared next to the name of the councilmember who I knew preferred the other candidate. But why the no vote from Councilman Smith? I thought he was clearly supportive of my candidacy.

After the mayor announced the appointment, the meeting concluded. After congratulatory handshakes and pats on the back, I walked down the hallway toward the council offices with Councilmember Smith. "Councilman," I asked, "what was that no vote all about? I thought you were going to support me." "Oh, that wasn't a no vote against you," he replied. "I voted no because I don't think we should have wasted $10,000 on an executive search when we could have just appointed you to the permanent position in May." I replied, "Wow, since you didn't say anything, it sure looked like a vote against me."

The following Monday, the city council met again for its weekly meeting. At the end of the agenda, during general council comments, Councilmember Smith addressed the appointment vote of the previous week. He said he would like the city council to reconsider the vote to appoint me as city manager. He further explained that since he had voted in the minority, Robert's Rules of Order prevented him from making the motion for reconsideration. He asked for one of the councilmembers who had voted for my appointment to make the motion. The councilmembers were looking at me for some reassurance that I knew what was going on. My look back at them made it clear that I didn't.

A motion and second were made to reconsider the appointment. Councilmember Smith explained the reasons for his previous week's vote and expressed his support for my appointment. A new motion and second were made to appoint me city manager, and the new vote was 4–1.

P.S. The local media announced the appointment with emphasis on my age (by then I had turned thirty-one). The lead paragraph in one local newspaper read something like this: "Council Appoints Tim Casey, Age 31, as New Redondo Beach City Manager. Based on his youthful appearance, it appears that Casey went directly from pablum to city planning." No, I am not kidding

Chapter 23

CAMP SNOOPY

LABOR NEGOTIATIONS WITH the police association had reached an impasse. First, the association staged a work slowdown. That wasn't particularly successful after an administrative analyst concluded that our police officers were writing more tickets and parking citations than the previous year. That prompted the association to stage a work speedup during which they dramatically increased citation activity. That caused the city council to question why our police officers hadn't always been that productive. Ultimately, the association staged a work sick-out.

None of these tactics had moved the city council, so the association hatched a new plan. As I arrived at city hall one morning, something unfamiliar struck me. The lawn in front of the council chambers was filled with pup tents and camping equipment. In its quest for higher wages, the police association had constructed this encampment to symbolize their plight and suggest that this was the only housing the police could afford.

The local news media (TV and print) loved it. In my first interview, they asked for my reaction. It was about that time that Knott's Berry Farm, a well-known and popular amusement park in Southern

California, had opened a new attraction, Camp Snoopy, named after the infamous cartoon beagle of Charles Schulz fame. Without much thought, I told the press that the police encampment reminded me of Camp Snoopy. The media grabbed it and reported that I had likened our police force to a bunch of juvenile theme park patrons.

The next day as I arrived at work, the camp was still there; however, there was a noticeable change. Overnight, someone with some lettering skills had wood-burned a name into a large piece of scrap redwood. The police association had affectionately dubbed its new homestead "Camp Casey."

Chapter 24

———— ❧ ————

BEACH BANNERS AND SKYLINES

THE LABOR DISPUTE with the police association was protracted. Camp Casey had come down, only to be replaced by off-duty officers, spouses, and children protesting and picketing the front entrance to city hall. Once again, the media descended.

In a particularly thoughtless moment, I agreed to an outside interview. After being properly positioned for the cameraman, the television news reporter encouraged all of the picketers to close in and chant around me. I did my best to express appreciation for the excellent work of our police officers and my hope that continued good faith negotiations would lead to a resolution of the labor dispute.

During the interview, someone yelled, "Look up, Tim." Flying overhead was one of those familiar biplanes that tow banners along the shoreline on sunny beach days hawking Coppertone Suntan Lotion or Corona beer. This one was different. The banner read, "Redondo Beach Police. First in Service. Last in Pay. Thanks, Tim."

The labor contract was settled soon thereafter.

P.S. Our regular weekly staff meeting was held the next day, and I was eager to get the reaction to my outdoor lawn interview from the executive team. After a brief pause, someone spoke for the group: "Sweat looks really gross on TV, Tim."

Chapter 25

———— ∾ ————

THE STRIPPER GOES AWOL

THE CITY COUNCIL agenda included a public comments section that allowed interested persons to address the council on non-agenda items. As I glanced out at the audience, I noticed Dan, one of our public works employees. However, he seemed heavier than I had remembered him.

When the mayor invited public comments, Dan approached the public microphone stand. Indeed, he did seem heavier and rather bulkily dressed. As he proceeded to air his grievances, he got louder and louder and punctuated his remarks with the continuous removal of his clothing: first his coat, then several shirts, and finally his pants.

With some concern about how far he might go, the ultimate outfit emerged. Beneath the multiple layers of clothing, he was dressed in a black leotard, gym shorts and a cape bearing the words "Sun Dog." "Don't mess with Sun Dog," he loudly proclaimed as he turned and scampered out the back door of the council chambers.

We never needed the services of the psychiatrist that the city retained to assess Dan's condition. He didn't report to work the next day or for several days thereafter. The city's Personnel Rules and Regulations contained an "abandonment of employment" provision which stated that five consecutive days of absence without approval constituted forfeiture of your position. After five days of waiting, we sent the official abandonment of employment notice to Dan's last known address. We never heard from him again.

Chapter 26

WHERE THERE'S A WILL, THERE'S A WAY

MARTIN WAS A park caretaker in the parks maintenance division of the Redondo Beach Public Works Department. The city had internally noticed that applications were being accepted for the promotional opportunity of senior parks caretaker, the next step up in the parks maintenance job series.

One afternoon, I noticed Martin waiting in the reception area of the city manager's office. "Mr. Casey, do you have a moment?" he asked. I invited Martin into my office, and he explained his interest in the senior park caretaker position. "That's great," I replied. "We'd welcome your application."

From the look on his face, I sensed something was wrong. "I don't think I can pass the written exam, Mr. Casey," Martin offered up. "I'm dyslexic and I can't read fast enough to complete the exam in one hour." But with confidence, he added, "But I really do know my stuff, Mr. Casey. With a little extra time, I know I can nail the test." He convinced me that he could, and I wanted to help him.

I contacted the union that represented the public works department employees and asked if they would consent to allowing Martin extra time to sit for the written exam. The union leadership did not think that would be fair to the other park caretakers seeking the promotional opportunity. I offered an alternative. Would they allow me to administer the questions verbally to Martin, record his answers, and limit the session to the one hour that others would be allowed? They said they would think about that and get back to me. After consideration, they consented.

On written examination day, Martin came to my office. We noted the start time, and I began reading the multiple-choice questions to Martin and marking his oral answers on the test sheet. The questions covered a variety of topics from park maintenance equipment to landscape maintenance methods to fertilizer and pesticide products and proper application. After hearing each question and the possible answers, Martin responded quickly and confidently. We finished the exam well before the allotted hour of time, and I pulled out the test key to check his results. Martin had scored 100 percent.

Martin was promoted to senior park caretaker. That was a good day.

P.S. Today, Martin is the Public Works Supervisor responsible for the maintenance of all parks in the City of Redondo Beach.

Chapter 27

SAVE OUR JOBS ... FIRE TIM!

AT THE TIME of my appointment as city manager, the City of Redondo Beach was still running a municipal residential refuse collection service. The observations of the Inglewood refuse superintendent remained valid. If there was any city service that must be provided come rain, snow, sleet, or hail, it was refuse collection. The trash must be picked up on schedule without interruption.

Just as he had predicted, the refuse collection operation often required the use of other public works employees from the parks and/or streets divisions. If too many refuse division employees were absent due to injury or illness, street maintenance workers and park caretakers would be impressed into service. The situation had reached the point where the public works director was requesting additional budgeted positions for the refuse division.

There was only one problem. Residential refuse collection rates in Redondo Beach were already significantly higher than those of other South Bay cities that had contracted the service out to private refuse collection companies. To make matters worse, the city council had never set refuse collection rates to reflect the true cost to the city, including general and departmental overhead. I suggested to the city council that it was time to get out of the refuse collection business and seek a qualified private hauler through a competitive process. Over the objections of refuse division employees and their union representatives, the council agreed.

We attempted to implement the council's decision in a thoughtful and professional way. Drawing from the experience of other South Bay cities, we drafted a comprehensive set of bid specifications, including minimum service, equipment, and performance requirements. During the drafting process, we froze vacant positions in the public works department to create transfer opportunities for affected refuse division employees. The final contract document also required the newly selected refuse collection company to offer a first right of refusal to displaced refuse division employees who would like to accept employment with the company.

The moment of reckoning had arrived. Competitive proposals had been received and staff was recommending that a multiyear contract be awarded to Western Waste, an established, reputable company headquartered in the nearby City of Carson. As I walked into the council chambers, the room was packed to standing-room-only capacity. It seemed that every public works employee was there in his or her orange OSHA work shirt, accompanied by their spouses and children. The protest signs read "Save Our Jobs...Fire Tim."

After seemingly endless testimony, the city council made the tough decision. The contract with Western Waste was approved, and the city was out of the refuse collection business. At the end of the meeting, we exited the council chambers, and it was a quiet walk down the hallway past the city council offices. Finally, one councilmember turned and said to me, "Please don't do that to us again." In my mind, I thought that this would probably not be the last time that I would make such a recommendation. It was becoming increasingly clear to me that a significant disparity was emerging between public and private sector compensation and that contracting out some city services was an option that many cities would need to consider in the future.

Chapter 28

THE $10 MILLION VERDICT

THE TRIANGLE SHOPPING Center was located on a triangular seven-and-a-half-acre parcel near the Redondo Beach waterfront. It was bounded on the long sides of the triangle by Hermosa and Pacific Avenues, and on the short side by Beryl Street. Purchased in 1947 by an investment group, a shopping center with about twenty stores was envisioned for this "modern" retail center. Early tenants included Mayfair Markets, Owl Rexall Drugs, and J. J. Newberry's.

Business was good in the 1950s and 1960s. However, the opening of South Bay Center in Redondo Beach and Del Amo Shopping Center in the neighboring City of Torrance took a toll. By the late 1970s, the Triangle Shopping Center's original anchor tenants had been replaced by an eclectic mix of businesses, including an antique market/swap meet, a couple of nightclubs featuring bluegrass music and punk rock bands, and an independent drug store. Fire ravaged a couple of businesses, leaving charred empty spaces.

Several private developers attempted to purchase the property, but their efforts were thwarted by the unusual ownership arrangement. Each business owned the pad underneath its building, but the parking lot was owned in common. It was seemingly impossible to get all owners to agree to a reasonable purchase price at the same time. One or more holdouts always frustrated the land acquisition process.

The property was truly blighted and a real eyesore on the city's developing waterfront harbor and pier area. The city council finally decided to formally declare the area as blighted and use its redevelopment agency powers to acquire the property. A request for development proposals was issued, and one of the city's existing harbor master lessees was selected to develop the property. His proposal envisioned a hotel and related uses.

The Redondo Beach Redevelopment Agency had the property appraised, and its fair market value was determined to be in the range of $5 million. An offer was made to the Triangle Shopping Center business/property owners, and they declined. One business owner in particular was defiant. He was not interested in selling his property and closing or relocating his business. His price demands were outrageously unrealistic.

Ultimately, the city council decided to use the redevelopment agency's power of condemnation (eminent domain) to acquire the property. Negotiations with the chosen lessee/developer led to an agreement that he would reimburse the agency for the land purchase up to an amount not to exceed $6.25 million. That provided a 25 percent cushion above the agency's appraised value of the land. The agency confidently proceeded to file an order for immediate possession that would allow the agency to seize the property and permit the hotel construction to proceed. In the event of a condemnation trial, we could not envision a judge or jury awarding a judgment that exceeded 125 percent of the appraised value. We were wrong.

The Triangle Shopping Center owners banded together and hired one of the most prominent condemnation defense lawyers in California. This guy had a tremendous track record on behalf of former clients and immediately requested a condemnation trial by jury. The role of the jury would be to review comparable property sales and determine its own fair market value for the property.

The Triangle Shopping Center was located near, but not immediately adjacent to, the Redondo Beach waterfront. It was separated from the closest water basin by a two-lane street, a large parking lot, and Seaside Lagoon, the city's outdoor, heated, saltwater swimming pool. A short distance to the north was the huge Southern California Edison power plant.

As the trial began, the condemnation defense lawyer offered up a list of recent coastal land sales intended for hotel use and development. One of the sites was an oceanfront, bluff-top property in South Orange County that was the proposed site of a Ritz Carlton Hotel. A visit to the property convinced us that it was far superior to the Redondo Beach hotel site and would not be considered by the jury. We were wrong again.

The jury used the South Orange County hotel site as the basis for its $10 million verdict. That was $3.75 million more than our lessee/developer was obligated to reimburse the redevelopment agency. Since the agency had already acquired the Triangle Shopping Center through the immediate possession order and hotel construction had begun, our only options were to appeal the jury's verdict or pay the piper. We chose the latter.

Fortunately, the city's Harbor Enterprise Fund had sufficient reserves to meet the funding gap, but it had been a colossal miscalculation. It was one of only two times in my city management career when I felt if I got fired, it would have been justified. Fortunately, I kept my job.

In January 1987, the 350-room Sheraton at Redondo Beach opened on the former Triangle Shopping Center site. A few years later, the hotel was acquired by the Holiday Inn group and rebranded as one of its Crowne Plaza Hotels. As of this writing, it continues to operate.

Chapter 29

———— ∼∼∼ ————

WHAT DMV LICENSE?

THE REDONDO BEACH Police Department had picked up a rumor that the South Bay Municipal Court judges were not happy with the private traffic violator schools that were being operated in the area. There was a belief that the certificates of completion were simply being mailed to registrants upon payment of the class fees and that the violators were not attending the mandatory eight hours of classroom instruction.

We saw an opportunity: let's open a city traffic violator school. We would staff it with the same traffic officers who wrote the tickets. As instructors, they would swap their uniforms and Ray-Ban sunglasses for civilian coats and ties in the classroom. We thought it would provide a chance for traffic violators to see law enforcement officers in a different light. It was also an extra income opportunity for our officers who would be paid overtime for an eight-hour day.

The judges loved the idea, and we launched the Redondo Beach Traffic School. We hired a Redondo Beach resident with an educational background to be the part-time program administrator. He and the police department developed an instructional curriculum that passed muster with the court. Classes were offered on Saturdays in the council chambers and initially drew thirty-five to fifty students per week who paid about fifty dollars for the course to have the traffic ticket removed from their record.

It seemed like a win-win situation for everybody. The judges had a credible traffic violator school that they trusted. Our police officers made a few extra bucks and got to interact with the students in an informal instructional setting. The program was increasingly popular, and soon the city was netting about $2,000 per week after expenses. Everyone seemed to like the program except the private traffic violator school operators…and, unfortunately, the California Department of Motor Vehicles.

The letter from the DMV looked rather ominous when it arrived in the mail. It was a cease and desist order. We were being shut down for illegally operating a traffic violator school without a license. Not a problem, I thought. We'll just shut down temporarily while we go through the licensing process. We applied for the license and were rejected. State law did not provide any authority for a city to operate a traffic violator school.

We briefly considered seeking special legislation but concluded that we would get hammered in Sacramento by the private operators. We quietly folded up shop.

It was fun while it lasted, and to this day, I still think it was a great idea.

Chapter 30

―――――∽∾∽―――――

THE FICKLE FINGER OF FATE

THE CONSENT CALENDAR was the part of the city council agenda where noncontroversial items and status reports were placed. It was usually approved in a single motion without discussion, although any member of the city council or the public could request that an item be pulled for separate consideration.

One of the routine monthly consent calendar items was a statistical report from the harbor director. It documented many items, including monthly harbor rents and revenues, parking structure vehicle counts and fees, special event attendance, and the like. It had been a part of the calendar before I became city manager, and I didn't recall anyone ever pulling it for separate consideration or asking a question about it.

On this night, the councilmember who represented the harbor/pier area pulled the statistical report from the consent calendar. He wasn't a fan of the way the harbor enterprise was being managed, and he wasn't a fan of the harbor director. He was also the councilmember who voted against my appointment as city manager.

He criticized the format of the report and questioned the accuracy of its content. I clearly remember his words: "Figures can lie and liars can figure," he started. Then he demanded a revision of the report in the future. Knowing that this councilmember was a minority voice on most harbor/pier issues, I responded to his criticism by confidently stating that the report was complete and accurate and that no changes would be made unless directed by a majority of the city council.

Feeling that I had adequately defended the harbor director and myself, I glanced into the staff section of the audience hoping to receive some sign of acknowledgment and appreciation from the harbor director. Instead, the department head was sitting in the front left row of the audience clearly extending his arm and middle finger to the councilmember.

I couldn't tolerate such conduct, and I summoned the harbor director to my office the next morning. I informed him that he was being suspended without pay for five days. He took the punishment in stride. Then, to my surprise, he asked if I could schedule the suspension during a specific week of his choosing to turn it into a three-week vacation opportunity. In the interest of decorum, I will not document my response.

Chapter 31

LOVE THY NEIGHBOR

SOUTH BAY CENTER had been one of the first open-air regional malls in Southern California when it opened in the 1950s. It was a single-story collection of retail shops anchored by a two-story May Company department store. However, over the years it had declined in appearance and competitive edge as newer shopping centers began to enter the market area.

The city was approached by an out-of-state developer and presented with two options. Without city financial assistance, the developer would buy the property and convert it into an off-price retail center with discount stores. With city assistance, the developer would buy the property and convert it into a first-class, three-story, state-of-the-art, atrium-lit super regional mall with a Nordstrom department store as the anchor tenant. No brainer here…the city opted for Nordstrom.

After evaluating public finance options, the development pro forma showed about a $10 million funding gap. The developer asked the city to apply for an Urban Development Action Grant, or UDAG. We were not familiar with UDAG, a federal economic development program, but agreed to look into it.

UDAGs were grants that cities could use to make loans to developers for projects. The loan would be repaid to the city, with interest, for continued use in the community. Cities were also encouraged to acquire an equity position in the project. Additionally, unemployed and underemployed city residents were given hiring priority for the newly created jobs.

It seemed like a good program, but there was one hitch. Redondo Beach was not an eligible UDAG applicant. The city did not have the required prerequisites of poverty, pre-World War II housing, etc. However, the neighboring City of Lawndale was on the eligible applicant list of California cities. Additionally, the Lawndale city boundary was adjacent to the shopping center site.

In an unprecedented effort, the Cities of Redondo Beach and Lawndale collaborated on the UDAG application. Lawndale was the official applicant and sought $10 million that would be loaned to the purchaser/developer of the Redondo Beach shopping center site. The City of Redondo Beach would benefit from the significant new sales tax revenue generated by the super regional mall. The City of Lawndale would be the beneficiary of the loan repayment proceeds, equity position in the project, and resident employment opportunities. Federal Department of Housing and Urban Development (HUD) officials found no precedent for such a joint application but did not discourage us. The application was submitted.

At the time the UDAG application was submitted, Redondo Beach was grappling with another issue. Dozens of day laborers were congregating each morning on a neighborhood corner in North Redondo to offer their services to interested contractors. The daily assemblage had reached nuisance proportion, and the residents wanted them ousted.

During a particularly heated city council meeting where relocation options were being discussed, the mayor burst out with an emotional and unexpected suggestion: "Why don't they just go someplace where they belong...like Lawndale?" I quietly left the council chambers during the meeting and walked to my office. I found my ICMA

Membership Directory and called the home telephone number of the Lawndale city manager. I described the mayor's comments and suggested that they would probably make the local newspapers. As I hung up, I wondered if our partnership and the $10 million UDAG application had just gone up in smoke.

My worst fears were realized. The Lawndale City Council did not take the comments well, and its mayor suggested it was time to reconsider the UDAG application. At first, there was a demand for a public apology, but after some behind-the-scenes diplomacy, cooler minds prevailed.

I took the phone call from Senator Pete Wilson with both excitement and anxiety. "Tim," he said, "I have some good news and some bad news. The bad news is that Lawndale didn't get the $10 million; the good news is that they got $8 million."

P.S. With the $8 million Urban Development Action Grant, the South Bay Galleria at Redondo Beach was built. Lawndale received the economic and employment benefits that were anticipated, and some years later the developer made a huge, one-time lump sum payment to the city representing the present value of the future income stream. Redondo Beach enjoyed the stature of host city for this beautiful new shopping center and the attendant sales tax benefits. In 1985, the Cities of Lawndale and Redondo Beach received the ICMA Award for Excellence in Community and Economic Development for this extraordinary public/public/private partnership.

Chapter 32

———～～———

Nixon versus Bozo

THE SOUTH BAY Union School High School District operated three high schools serving the Cities of Redondo Beach, Hermosa Beach, and Manhattan Beach. Mira Costa High School was located in Manhattan Beach, while Redondo Union High School and Aviation High School were both located in Redondo Beach.

In 1981, due in large part to budget constraints and declining enrollment, the district's board of trustees determined it would be necessary to close one of the three high schools. With two of the schools located in Redondo Beach, it seemed inevitable that one of them would be shuttered. After deliberation by a twenty-one-member citizen's advisory committee and numerous public hearings, the board voted in 1982 to close Aviation High School.

The closure prompted some challenging and complex negotiations between the city and the district regarding the rezoning of the forty-acre site and the preservation of the sports and recreational facilities that had become an important part of the fabric of the city. Those facilities included a night-lighted football stadium and running track, a 1,400-seat auditorium, a double gymnasium, and an abandoned indoor swimming pool.

The forty-acre site was bounded on two sides by two major streets: Aviation Boulevard and Manhattan Beach Boulevard. The other two sides were bounded by portions of TRW's Space and Defense Systems facility. As such it seemed logical to rezone most of the school site for research-and-development uses.

The city and district worked together to develop a logical parcel map to divide the portions of the site that would be permitted for R&D uses from the portion of the site where existing recreational facilities would be preserved. Most, but not all, of the recreational amenities would remain and a three-acre parking lot would be preserved.

While the city and district moved forward, a group of residents introduced its own zoning initiative to preserve all of the recreational facilities on the property. Their proposed zoning map wrapped an irregular, multisided polygon around the eleven acres of sports facilities, but excluded the three-acre parking lot. After circulating petitions, the group gathered enough signatures to place its zoning proposal on the ballot. The city and district had no choice but to place our collaborative zoning plan on the ballot as a competing measure.

The ballot results proved the old adage that every vote counts. Both measures were approved by the voters. In California, when two competing ballot measures pass, the one with the most yes votes prevails. After the first count, the public initiative led by a small margin of votes. The school district paid for a recount. After the second count, the public initiative led by a handful of votes. The school district sought one more recount. After the third count, the public initiative led by three votes. That was it, and the final election results were certified.

It was now up to the city and district to figure out how to implement the voters' will. Negotiations continued on issues ranging from how much private development would be permitted on the site to how the city would acquire the sports and recreational facilities. The fate of the three-acre parking lot also had to be determined. It occupied the prime corner of Aviation and Manhattan Beach Boulevards and was a valuable piece of real estate.

A negotiating session was scheduled for Halloween in the district superintendent's office, which was located just across Pacific Coast Highway within walking distance of city hall. It was my practice to join the fun on Halloween and dress up with the rest of the city hall employees. I was in full clown costume with face makeup and a wig as I crossed Pacific Coast Highway at Diamond Street and approached the school district offices.

When I entered the superintendent's office, his executive secretary just about fell out of her chair. Trying to keep a straight face, she escorted me into the office. The superintendent (Hugh) and the three members of the district's real estate consulting team (Bill, Claudia, and Chris) were already seated awaiting my arrival. They were all dressed in formal business attire.

After a few strange looks and giggles, our serious discussion ensued. We worked through key issues marking tentative agreement on some issues and promising to come back to some of the sticking points. After thirty to forty-five minutes, Chris interrupted. "I'm sorry," he said, "but I just can't negotiate with a clown. I'll be right back."

When Chris returned, we all had a good laugh. He had gone to his car and retrieved an item from his trunk. He walked back into the room wearing a perfect rubber President Richard Nixon mask with his business suit. Negotiations resumed.

P.S. The city and district reached agreement on the disposition of the former Aviation High School site. The city acquired the eleven-acre sports and recreation area and facilities for one dollar. The city's parking authority acquired the three-acre public parking lot for its appraised fair market value. The remaining twenty-six acres was rezoned for research-and-development uses, and the district ground-leased the property to a Southern California developer who constructed a 550,000-square-foot R&D office park. TRW quickly entered into leases for the new office space.

Chapter 33

———— ∼∼∼ ————

YOU'RE NOT A LAWYER OR A CPA?

DOUG WAS A prominent Los Angeles real estate attorney. I had met him during the negotiations on the reuse and redevelopment of the shuttered Aviation High School site. He represented the development firm that won the ground lease rights to the property and developed the 550,000-square-foot research-and-development park that was subsequently leased by TRW.

Doug and I had an enjoyable professional working relationship on the project, and I think he appreciated my management and problem-solving style. Doug's father was a well-known property owner in Los Angeles County. He had pioneered the concept of developing large garden apartments for young couples and had built more than five thousand units over four decades.

By the early 1970s, most of the properties had been sold, but Doug's father still owned a holding company that owned several luxury apartment buildings in the upscale Marina Del Rey harbor and waterfront area of Los Angeles County. While Doug's father was the president/CEO of the holding company, there was an executive vice president who managed day-to-day operations.

Doug called one day to inform me that the executive vice president position was open. "So what's that to me?" I asked. "I think you would be a great candidate for the position," Doug replied. "But I don't know anything about apartment management," I responded. Doug went on to convince me that I had many transferable skills for the executive VP position. The City of Redondo Beach was a master landlord over seventeen leasehold estates in the Pier and King Harbor area. The city owned and maintained many buildings: city hall, the police station, two fire stations, and two libraries. The city also owned and maintained numerous parks and recreational facilities, and it ran recreation programs for thousands of residents. "Oh, there is one thing," Doug added. "All of Dad's previous executive vice presidents have either been a lawyer or a certified public accountant."

After Doug vouched for me, his father invited me to a personal interview at his Bel Air home. I drove to his swank neighborhood of multimillion dollar homes, parked my car, and made my way toward the front door. The home was beautiful, and I had to walk on a narrow bridge over a shallow pool of water to the front porch. I rang the doorbell, the door opened, and Doug's dad appeared. He was a smartly dressed gentleman in his midsixties. I introduced myself and shook his hand as he invited me inside.

We settled comfortably in his living room, and he began to describe the duties and responsibilities of the executive vice president position. When it was my turn, I described my educational background and city management experience. As I spoke, it was clear to me that he was having some difficulty seeing any relevant relationship between the role of a city manager and the duties and responsibilities of his executive vice president. I explained that as city manager of the City of Redondo Beach, I was the chief executive officer of a $40 million, multiservice corporation. I did my best to draw some parallels between the two positions, drawing upon the examples that Doug had provided in our earlier phone conversation.

At the completion of my remarks, Doug's father had two comments.

"So, you're not a lawyer," he said. "No, I am not," I replied. "And you're not a CPA," he continued. "No, I am not," I responded. "Well, it's been nice meeting you, Tim," he concluded, and that was the end of the interview.

I later learned from Doug that his father hired either another lawyer or certified public accountant for the position.

Chapter 34

THE REAL ESTATE COUNTEROFFER

WHEN I WAS appointed city manager of Redondo Beach in 1981, Roz and I were living in the neighboring City of Torrance. Shannon was only six months old.

As a bachelor, I had purchased the nine-hundred-square-foot, three-bedroom and one-bath home in 1976 for $51,500. I induced my two apartment roommates to move with me by offering to reduce their rent by twenty-five dollars per month. It was a sweet deal. Their rent covered nearly half of my monthly mortgage payment, and I was receiving the property appreciation and tax benefits of home ownership.

Nine years into my city management career, I had developed strong feelings that, if possible, the city manager should live in the city that he/she was managing. The city council and I had discussed that possibility at the time of my promotion but couldn't come to terms. They weren't willing to offer financial assistance for relocation, and I just couldn't make it pencil out even with my salary increase. Nonetheless, over the next few years I would keep my eyes open for For Sale signs as I drove through Redondo Beach neighborhoods.

The house for sale at 410 Avenue E caught my eye. It was a

single-story ranch-style home with some curb appeal. The "avenues" section of southern Redondo Beach was a desirable place to live within walking distance of Riviera Village and the ocean. I took Roz on a drive-by. The home was listed for $209,000, and we felt we could make a competitive offer based on the value of our Torrance home which had climbed to about $175,000.

There was only one potential impediment. It turned out that the home was owned by one of our Redondo Beach police lieutenants. After consulting with the city attorney, it was concluded that there was no potential conflict of interest if the city manager purchased a home owned by another city employee. It was just necessary that it be a fair-market-value, arms-length transaction carried out through our respective real estate agents.

The offer and counteroffer process began. We offered $201,000, contingent upon the sale of our Torrance home. The lieutenant and his wife countered at $207,000 and accepted our contingency. We countered at $203,000, still contingent on the sale of our Torrance home.

The phone call came from our real estate agent. He wanted to come by the house with the written counteroffer from the lieutenant. He said that our offer of $203,000 had been accepted, but the sellers had added two conditions to the sale that he did not fully understand.

When he arrived at the house, he handed me the counteroffer document. I glanced down at the handwritten counterproposal which read:

1. The Caseys' offer of $203,000 is accepted.
2. All Redondo Beach police lieutenants shall receive an immediate 1 percent salary increase.
3. The seller shall be promoted to police captain within one year.

"Now that's really funny," I thought. I explained to the real estate agent that it was a joke, and he seemed relieved. Roz and I listed our house in Torrance for $176,500 and left town for a conference. When we returned a few days later, we had three full-price offers. Not long after that, Roz, Shannon, and I were in our new home in Redondo Beach.

Chapter 35

I KNOW WHAT JOB YOU DIDN'T GET

I HAD BEEN city manager of the City of Redondo Beach for a few years. While I was happy in the position, felt I was doing a good job, and was not seeking a change, occasionally another opportunity would catch my eye. When a vacancy occurred in a larger, full-service Southern California beach city, I decided to throw my name in the hat and test my competitiveness.

I updated my résumé, prepared my cover letter, and submitted both to the personnel department of the city. The other beach city had a good reputation for professional city management, and the previous city manager had served in the position for many years. I felt that my experience and our accomplishments in Redondo Beach would make me a strong candidate, and I was confident that I would be invited for the first interview.

It was the weekend, and I was doing some work in the front yard of our new Redondo Beach home when the mailman parked his truck in front of the house. After delivering the mail to our next-door neighbor, he walked onto our driveway double-checking the letters and magazines in his hand. I walked over to greet him and accept the mail. As he approached, he pulled a postcard from the batch and loudly proclaimed, "Oh, I know what job you didn't get." With that, he handed me our mail and headed back to his truck.

The postcard was from the city where I had applied to be city manager. It was stamped, postmarked, and addressed to me on one side of the card. The other side was printed in a standard format and read something like this:

Dear _____. Thank you for your interest in the position of _____. We had many outstanding applicants for the position of _____. Regretfully, we cannot provide an interview opportunity for the many qualified candidates, and your application will not receive further consideration. Thank you again for your interest in employment with the city, and we wish you the best in your future endeavors.

Handwritten in ink in the first blank were the words "Mr. Casey." Handwritten in ink in the second and third blanks were the words "City Manager."

"Are you kidding me?" I thought. "This is the way that they notify and reject candidates for their chief executive officer position?" It was the last city manager position that I applied for until seeking the position of first city manager for the City of Laguna Niguel in Orange County, California.

Chapter 36

———— ∾ ————

Now You See Him ... Now You Don't

I HAD BECOME increasingly frustrated with the performance of the city library director. He was a veteran member of the city's executive team whom I had inherited upon my appointment as city manager. His office was located in the main library in Veterans Park, a few blocks away from city hall.

The city council was interested in exploring options for a new library. Redondo Union High School was located across Pacific Coast Highway from city hall. One option was to explore the cost and feasibility of siting and building a joint high school and municipal library on the Redondo Union High School campus in partnership with the South Bay Union High School District. I tasked the library director with the responsibility of conducting the administrative research on this option and reporting back with his findings and recommendations by the end of the fiscal year. It was his only significant work program assignment for the year.

As city manager, I expected department heads to carry out their work program assignments with minimal direction or supervision. If they needed some guidance from me, they should request it. It wasn't my management style to keep regular tabs on their work or request periodic progress reports. In retrospect, I probably should have been more diligent in that respect.

As the fiscal year was ending, I asked the library director if he had concluded his research and was ready to deliver his findings and recommendations. He stated that he was, and we scheduled an appointment for him to come to my office. When he arrived at my office, I expected to see him carrying one or more copies of his report. Instead, he came in carrying a small green book.

"Here," he said, "read this. I agree with all of its findings and conclusions." As I opened the book, it seemed to be a little old and dusty. Upon further examination, I realized that it was some student's library science master's degree thesis from the 1930s. The topic of the thesis was an evaluation of the pros and cons of combining public school and municipal libraries. The graduate student author of the thesis had concluded that a combined school/municipal library was neither feasible nor practical.

On the inside, I was furious. The library director had not taken his work assignment seriously and had not initiated any original research or analysis during the entire year. I made my displeasure with his unsatisfactory performance clearly known.

Staff meetings were held weekly on Wednesday mornings. At the next meeting, the library director was absent, but his senior librarian was in attendance. I didn't think much about it. At the next week's meeting, the library director was again absent, and the senior librarian again attended. When the same thing happened at the following week's meeting, I asked the senior librarian where her boss was. She meekly responded, "We thought maybe you knew."

Phone calls to the library director's home went unanswered; the line had been disconnected. A visit to his place of residence suggested that no one was living there. In pondering the possible explanations, a question occurred to me: "Could an employee retire without the city knowing about it?" I asked the personnel department to contact the

California Public Employees Retirement System (PERS) to see if they knew anything. Indeed, the now former library director was a newly retired PERS annuitant. We never could figure out how that happened without the city being contacted or notified.

Chapter 37

———— ❧ ————

I WOULD NEVER SAY THAT TO YOU

THERE HAD BEEN some turnover on the city council, so I suggested that a team-building retreat might be a good idea. The League of California Cities had contracted with an experienced facilitator who conducted such retreats twice per year, one in Northern California at Fallen Leaf Lake and one in Southern California at Lake Arrowhead. We opted for the Southern California location, about a two-hour drive from Redondo Beach.

Four of us agreed to attend: the mayor, a councilman, a council-woman, and me. Since there were only four of us, we decided to car-pool, and the councilman offered to drive. The trip up the mountain was beautiful, and everyone was congenial. When we arrived at the Lake Arrowhead Conference Center, we checked in, carted our lug-gage to our rooms, and headed to a conference room for the opening session. Our city was one of several that had sent delegations for the team-building experience.

The first afternoon focused on getting to know each other better. There were some exercises to break the ice and learn more about our personal backgrounds. Where were you born and raised? Where did you go to school? What jobs have you held? How many kids do you have and how old are they?

Toward the close of the afternoon, we were asked to share something about ourselves that the others were unlikely to know. I remember the councilwoman proudly telling us that she had built a car engine from scratch...and it worked! I told them that in my golfing prime, I had scored a one-over-par 72 at Los Verdes Golf Course on the Palos Verdes Peninsula in Los Angeles County. I was two under par through thirteen holes, and then I jinxed myself, thinking that if I could finish with five straight pars, I would shoot a 69. I bogeyed three of the last five holes. The afternoon went smoothly, and we enjoyed a nice dinner together.

The next morning, we got down to the serious business. The facilitator led us through an exercise. The first step was to write a note to each person listing three things that he or she did that helped you perform your duties well and effectively. The notes were positive and encouraging, and everyone felt good about the messages.

The second step was to write another note to each person listing three things that you wish they would stop doing or do differently to help you perform your job better. We completed the assignment, exchanged our notes, and read them to ourselves. As we prepared to discuss the notes, the facilitator yelled, "That's it. We're out of time. I'll see you all in fifteen minutes for our concluding luncheon."

When we reconvened in the dining room for lunch, there were only three of us: the mayor, the councilman, and me. We waited for about fifteen minutes, but the councilwoman never joined us. The mayor offered to go to her room and make sure everything was all right. A few minutes later, the mayor returned and said, "We have a problem. Come with me."

We quickly exited the dining room and made our way to the councilwoman's room. She was lying on her bed crying her eyes out. As we entered the room, she looked up at us and scolded, "I would never say those things to you." It turns out that our messages had not been received as constructive criticism, and she was clearly hurt.

We packed our bags and loaded into the councilman's car for the trip home. No one uttered a word. It was the longest two hours of my life.

P.S. About a year later, I decided it was time to try team building again. However, this time I decided to serve as the facilitator. The mayor, city council, and I were scheduled to attend a conference at a Southern California hotel. We set aside an afternoon to meet in one of our hotel rooms to work on improving our working relationships and begin charting city goals and objectives for the upcoming fiscal year. As I departed my hotel room for the team-building session, my wife opined that this was going to be another disaster. My wife is a very smart woman. There was a lot of yelling, blaming, and finger pointing; fortunately, nobody died.

Chapter 38

———∾∾———

OUCH, THAT HURT!

THE FIRST FIVE months of 1988 were filled with tragedy and sadness in Redondo Beach. A dreadful accident at the annual Super Bowl Sunday 10K Run had left several race participants critically injured and one dead. In April, a rogue spring storm brought twenty-foot ocean waves crashing into the King Harbor area. The federal breakwater was severely damaged, and the popular Blue Moon Saloon restaurant was destroyed. The Portofino Inn hotel pad was severed from its adjacent land mass, the south portion of the building collapsed, and one-third of its rooms were destroyed. Guests had to be evacuated by helicopter. In May, the city's landmark pier caught fire. Seventeen businesses were destroyed, and five hundred feet of the historic wooden pier structure were lost.

The phone at home rang at about eleven o'clock that night. I answered. "Is this Tim?" a male voice asked. "Yes, it is," I replied. "Tim, this is Senator Pete Wilson. I'm in San Diego and want to fly by helicopter to Redondo Beach in the morning to survey your harbor and pier damage. Can you contact the mayor and city council and meet me on the beach south of the pier at around ten a.m.?" "Yes, Senator. We'll be there," I promised.

As I made the late evening calls to the mayor and city council, it was clear that we would need several cars to drive to the beach to meet the senator. The next morning, I rode in a police vehicle with the police chief and the councilwoman who represented the harbor and pier area. We had a driver, so the three of us were in the back seat. The police chief was seated by the left door, I was by the right door, and the councilwoman was in the middle.

Our driver parked the car on the concrete bike path south of the pier, and we waited for Senator Wilson's arrival. As the helicopter approached from a distance, we waited in the car for the aircraft to land, the sandstorm to settle, and the copter blades to stop. When we saw Senator Wilson step out of the helicopter, I enthusiastically exited the car to greet him. Slamming the door behind me, I heard an immediate cracking sound and a terrible scream. I had slammed the door on the councilwoman's wrist.

The X-rays were conclusive. I had broken her arm.

I learned a lot that week about the workers' compensation status of local elected officials. I also had chauffeuring duty to and from the councilwoman's home to city council meetings for the next six weeks. I guess that also fell under the category of "other duties as required."

Chapter 39

Burn, Baby, Burn!

After the destructive storms of January and April 1988, I was looking forward to a little recreation. Jim H. and Jim C. worked for the city's insurance broker who helped us secure our employee health insurance coverage. Greg was the account executive for our health insurance provider. All of us played golf, and they had invited me to join them for an eighteen-hole round at Monarch Beach Golf Links in South Orange County.

It was the Friday before Memorial Day weekend. We met for an early lunch at the course before embarking on our afternoon round. We completed the front nine and were about halfway through the second nine on the fourteenth hole. It was an uphill par four. I had hit a poor drive, and my second shot left me in the fairway about ninety yards from the green.

As I sized up my third shot and addressed the ball, I was distracted by something out of the corner of my eye. When I looked back, I saw a course marshal approaching rapidly in his golf cart with a walkie-talkie radio in his hand. "Is Tim Casey in this group?" he yelled as he got closer. "That's me," I replied. "Your mayor is on the phone with our head pro," he continued. "She wants you to know that the Redondo Beach Pier is on fire." "Well, what in the hell does she expect me to do about it?" I thought, clearly annoyed.

Hearing the news, my golfing buddies asked if we needed to quit the round so I could return to the city. "Nope," I responded. "We're going to complete all eighteen holes." With that, I returned to my ball, executed my swing, and watched the ball soar toward the green. One bounce…two bounces…and it rolled into the hole for a birdie three. As my buddies ran over to exchange high fives, one of them loudly yelled, "Burn, baby, burn!"

The pre-Memorial Day weekend traffic was heavy that afternoon. It took me about three hours to make my way back to Redondo Beach. When I arrived at the pier, the press conference was concluding. As I walked into the assembled crowd, I heard the councilwoman who represented the harbor/pier area promise those in attendance, "Just as the famous phoenix, the pier will rise from its ashes." And, of course, it did.

Chapter 40

———— ∾ ————

YOU CAN BUILD IT
ANYWHERE BUT THERE

IN APRIL 1988, twenty-foot storm-driven waves caused severe damage to the Redondo Beach King Harbor breakwater, buildings, and boats. One of the casualties was the Blue Moon Saloon, a popular restaurant and bar perched on the water's edge, separated from the ocean by only a narrow pedestrian walkway and a short rock revetment.

The restaurant was destroyed. A rogue wave came crashing through the restaurant's seaward windows. It was a total loss. Not surprisingly, lawsuits followed alleging that the city had not taken appropriate action to protect the Blue Moon Saloon, and other damaged businesses, from destructive storms and waves.

By the time I arrived in Laguna Niguel as the first city manager, the lawsuits stemming from the 1988 storms and pier fire were still pending. I spent many days and countless hours appearing for depositions scheduled by the plaintiffs' lawyers. Numerous public record requests had been filed with the City of Redondo Beach searching for all documents related to the original development of King Harbor and the protective federal breakwaters. The breakwaters (the long upper breakwater and the shorter lower breakwater) had been designed and constructed by the United States Army Corps of Engineers. This multiyear process began with preliminary siting and reconnaissance studies followed by preliminary design and engineering, final design and engineering, and award of a construction contract.

The public record requests yielded the discovery of a significant and unwelcome engineering report. The upper and lower breakwaters were designed and positioned in a manner to allow safe boat entry and exit from the marina areas while protecting the land and building areas—at least most of the land and building areas. The engineering report unearthed from the basement storage area of city hall contained a cautionary note. It pinpointed one area of land that would not be protected from a major storm and waves. If it had been a treasure map where X marked the spot of the buried treasure, the X in the engineering report fell right on the spot where the Blue Moon Saloon restaurant had been constructed.

It is my recollection that at least one lawsuit was quickly settled by the city and its insurers.

Chapter 41

———⚊⚊⚊———

THE $10 MILLION VIDEO

THE REDONDO BEACH Main Library was built in the 1930s. It was a beautiful oceanside structure within Veteran's Park and had been placed on the National Register of Historic Places. Unfortunately, the building was not seismically reinforced.

By the 1980s, it had become clear that the library was woefully inadequate for our community of over sixty thousand people. The search began for a new site and a funding source for a new, modern, state-of-the-art library and media center. Property became available next to city hall, and the city began the acquisition process.

In 1988, California voters approved a state library bond act. The first funding cycle included $20 million in grant funds that would be awarded on a competitive basis. City staff scrambled to put together a first-cycle grant application documenting the history and substandard conditions of the main library.

A member of the city's executive team wisely suggested that we put together a video tour of the library as part of the grant application. I thought that was a great idea and authorized the expenditure. The last shot in the video was of a patron standing at the urinal in the men's room doing his business as books flew toward his feet onto the bathroom floor. This was not contrived; the night book drop was located on the outside wall of the men's room.

I had moved on to the city manager's position for the City of Laguna Niguel, Orange County, when the 1988 State Library Bond Act grant awards were announced. The City of Redondo Beach had been awarded $10 million of the $20 million in available grant funds and proceeded with the construction of a forty-thousand-square-foot library/media center on the property next to city hall. The state library staff cited the video as the key to their funding decision.

P.S. In 2002, California voters approved a new $330 million library bond act. Orange County Public Library staff and I attended a state workshop on the new bond program to explore the possible replacement or expansion of the Laguna Niguel Branch Library. State library staff explained the minimum application requirements. They then specifically mentioned the Redondo Beach video that had helped secure the $10 million from the 1988 grant program. I am sure they had no idea that anybody in the audience that day would be familiar with the story until I sheepishly raised my hand and said, "That was my city and our urinal."

Chapter 42

You're Late ... and You're Hired

In fall **1989,** I got a call from Greg, the account executive for the city's health insurance provider who lived in the community of Laguna Niguel in South Orange County, California. Greg informed me that the community was going to vote in November on whether Laguna Niguel would become Orange County's twenty-ninth city. "So why are you calling me?" I asked. "Well," said Greg, "I guess if we become a city, we're going to need a city manager." I thanked Greg for the information.

At that time, I had been the city manager of Redondo Beach for over eight years. I had used up a few of my nine lives, but things were still going well. I was happy in the job and not seeking new city management opportunities.

In spring 1990, the flyer arrived. The inaugural Laguna Niguel City Council was recruiting its first city manager. I took a quick glance at the flyer and placed it on my credenza in the stack of papers that I always intended to look at later but never did.

A few weeks later, the phone rang. It was a principal of the executive search firm that was handling the recruitment for the young new city. "Tim, did you see the recruitment brochure for Laguna Niguel?" he asked. "Yes," I said, "but I'm really not interested. I'm happy where I am." "Tim," he continued, "I really think you ought to submit your résumé. I think you are perfectly suited for the position." I found that strange. I was familiar with the executive search firm and the recruiter, but we had never met. "We don't even know each other," I responded. "You don't know me, but it's my job to know you," he responded. He persisted in his insistence that I apply for the position, and I promised him that I would, mostly to end the conversation. I updated my résumé, drafted a cover letter, and dropped them in the mail.

A few days later, the phone rang. It was the recruiter again. "Congratulations," he greeted. "You're a finalist for the position." I asked, "How can that be?" He informed me that the mayor and city council were very impressed with my professional background, especially my work and accomplishments in Redondo Beach. They wanted me to appear for a personal interview. I agreed to meet with them.

In preparation for the interview, Roz and I drove from Redondo Beach to Laguna Niguel to check out the new city. We had passed Laguna Niguel traveling to and from San Diego on the I-5 Freeway but had never spent any time in the community. I had played golf at the Monarch Beach Golf Links, which had been part of the Laguna Niguel community, but ultimately ended up within the adjoining new City of Dana Point. Roz and I turned right onto Crown Valley Parkway passing through an older commercial/industrial area before entering the heart of this master-planned community. It was beautiful: shiny new homes with red-tiled roofs, neatly landscaped slopes and street medians, new shopping centers. As we continued down Crown Valley Parkway, it didn't take long for Roz to declare, "You've got to get this job. I want to live here." No pressure.

The first interview was scheduled for a Friday at 5:00 p.m. at the new city hall, which was rented space in an industrial office park. I allotted two hours driving time from Redondo Beach to Laguna Niguel. It wasn't enough. About one hour into the drive south, I knew I wasn't going to make it in time. This was pre-cell phone days, so my only choice was to get off the freeway and find a payphone or keep trudging on. I chose the latter.

As I pulled into the city hall parking lot, I saw a tall gentleman with dark hair peering out a back-door entrance. "Are you Casey?" he yelled. "Yes, I am," I replied. "Well, get your ass in here," he responded. I shook his hand and apologized for my tardiness as he escorted me into a back conference room. There, I exchanged introductions with the mayor and other councilmembers.

Given my tardiness, the interview began around 5:10 p.m. I felt I was well-prepared. I had spent hours reviewing city council agendas and minutes, reading copies of the weekly community newspaper, and speaking anonymously with various community leaders and stakeholders. Questions were asked, and my answers flowed smoothly and confidently. At 5:50 p.m., the mayor politely ended the interview to allow the council to prepare for the next candidate. I thanked them for the opportunity to present myself and told them I could find my way back to the entrance door. As I departed, there was another candidate waiting for his opportunity. I did not know him, but we wished each other well.

On the way home, two things occurred to me. First, I was kicking myself in the behind for being late, thereby depriving myself of the full interview time. Second, I realized that I had not felt any personal chemistry with the group, individually or collectively. Upon arriving home, I informed Roz that it had been a valuable experience, but I did not think we would be hearing from the city again.

It was budget preparation time, and I found myself in the office the next day, a Saturday. Shortly after I arrived, the phone rang. It was Roz. The executive search firm recruiter had just called the house and wanted to talk to me. Roz said he was waiting in his office for a call back. I rang his number, and he quickly answered the phone.

"Congratulations," he said. "They want you for the position." I replied, "How can that be? I only met with them for forty minutes and I didn't feel any chemistry." "What do you want to do?" he asked. After a few moments of thought, I responded, "I want some quality time to meet with them again, probably a couple of hours."

Roz and I returned to Laguna Niguel for the second meeting. I told her it would probably last about two hours and she should spend that time driving around the community and scouting residential areas. When she returned, she sat in the parking lot for another two hours. My second meeting and conversation with the mayor and city council spanned nearly four hours. At its conclusion, it was apparent that the mayor and city council wanted me as the city's first chief executive. I told them I wanted to sleep on their offer and discuss it more with Roz. The mayor indicated that she would follow up with me the next day.

The next morning, the phone rang rather early. It was the mayor calling to see if I had made a decision. I told her I was interested in accepting the position, subject to negotiation of acceptable terms and conditions of employment. She was delighted and directed me to submit my proposed compensation terms to the city council through the recruiter.

I contacted the recruiter to discuss the proposed compensation package. He suggested that this would be my most advantageous moment in the negotiation process and to ask for what I really wanted. At the time, my base salary was $102,000 per year. I didn't want to appear greedy, but my research had convinced me that our cost of housing was going to increase even if we purchased a home in the price range of our house in Redondo Beach. We would likely be faced with a higher mortgage interest rate as well as higher property taxes and homeowner's association fees. I asked for a starting salary of $102,000 plus a housing allowance of $700 per month.

The recruiter conveyed my requests to the city council and quickly got back to me. "I've got some good news and bad news," he reported. "The city council wants you to take a salary cut. They don't want their first significant personnel hire to yield a six-figure headline in the local newspapers. The good news is that they accept your housing allowance proposal. Oh, and there's something else. They want you and Roz to quickly find a rental home or townhome in Laguna Niguel so Shannon can start school with the rest of the kids in the fall. They are willing to cover a lease of up to six months while you find your permanent home in the city." "Wow," I thought to myself, "they drive a hard bargain."

The deal was sealed. I started as Laguna Niguel's city manager in August 1990. Roz and I leased a townhome in the Marina Hills community and our family relocated. Shannon started fourth grade at George White Elementary School that September. The school had just opened prior to the close of the previous school year, so all of the kids were new to the school. As we stood in line with the other parents and students on the first day of school, we were greeted by Shannon's new teacher. She was sweet and wearing a Laura Ashley dress. At that moment, we knew everything was going to be all right.

P.S. At the end of the recruitment and selection process, I drafted my job acceptance letter and sent it to the consultant who had been serving as interim city manager after the city's incorporation. A few days after I dropped it in the mail, I called him to confirm its delivery. "Hi, Dan," I started. "Did you get my acceptance letter and forward it to the city council? "Yes, I got it," he replied, "but I didn't forward it to the city council." "Why?" I asked. "Do you have a copy handy?" he replied. "Read the last sentence."

I looked at my copy and read the last sentence: "In closing, I look forward to the opportunity to serve the mayor, city council, residents, and businesses of the City of Laguna **Beach**." Great start, Tim. I quickly corrected and signed a new letter and dropped it in the mail.

Chapter 43

WHAT NINETY-SIX ACRES OF PARKLAND?

I HAD ACCEPTED the position of city manager of the new City of Laguna Niguel. The terms and conditions of employment had been negotiated, and the unsigned employment agreement was sitting on my desk in Redondo Beach.

The phone rang, and it was former Redondo Beach City Manager Dave Dolter, my predecessor. After his abrupt resignation, Dave had gone to work for a Canadian-based residential developer and had relocated to Northern California to oversee a project. He told me he had heard I had been offered the Laguna Niguel job and wanted to know if I had sealed the deal. When I told him that the unsigned employment agreement was sitting on my desk, he cautioned me to think twice and dig a little deeper. He mentioned something about a district attorney's investigation and some missing parkland.

I called the city attorney to inquire. He took a minute to close his office door and returned to his phone. "How in the hell do you know about that?" he blurted out. "The DA's office just arrived with trucks this week and carted out boxes of files from city hall." Dave had been right. There was an allegation involving the Laguna Niguel Community Services District and members of the new city council regarding ninety-six acres of open space and parkland being improperly given back to a developer.

The Laguna Niguel Community Services District (LNCSD) was an independent special district that was established a few years prior to Laguna Niguel's incorporation as a city. It was responsible for providing limited local government services to Laguna Niguel residents, including park and landscape maintenance, recreation programs, street sweeping, and street lighting. Four of its five board members had been elected to the inaugural city council, and the city had assumed responsibility for the LNCSD services.

Over the next eighteen months, the city attorney, the community development director, and I tried to piece together the puzzle of the allegedly missing parkland. At the same time, the Orange County Grand Jury launched its own investigation.

The parkland that was allegedly missing was within the Marina Hills residential area and the adjacent Salt Creek Corridor, a huge open-space area. At the end of our staff investigation, our findings were quite simple. Prior to incorporation, the Avco Development company had received subdivision approvals from the County of Orange to develop the Marina Hills residential area. The original subdivision maps included offers of parkland and open space totaling about ninety-six acres. Since the LNCSD was responsible for parks and open-space maintenance, the irrevocable offers of dedication were made to the district, not the county.

After the county approvals, Avco sold its property and entitlement rights to another developer, Taylor Woodrow (TW). TW had other residential development plans for the area and processed new subdivision maps through the county. Their new subdivision proposal included 102 acres of parkland and open space, including several fully developed neighborhood park sites and amenities. The district/city had actually netted six additional acres of parkland and open space.

So what was the basis for the ninety-six-acre allegation? As it turned out, the Laguna Niguel Community Services District had never accepted the irrevocable offer of dedication (IOD) of the acreage, but legal counsel had concluded that the district should take formal action to vacate its interest in the unaccepted IOD. An item was placed on the LNCSD agenda as a consent calendar item to approve a quitclaim deed. The written staff report was not particularly descriptive or informative, which probably caught the eye of some curious district watchdogs. However, the recommendation was approved unanimously. When it was time for a district officer to execute the quitclaim deed, the board president was not available, and the document was signed by the board vice president. Apparently, this was somewhat unprecedented, although perfectly proper. However, the board vice president was also married to a real estate agent who later did some work for Taylor Woodrow. The conspiracy theories were launched.

The city attorney, community development director, and I thought we had done an excellent job of unraveling and describing the ninety-six-acre puzzle. A press conference was conducted at city hall where we worked methodically through the facts and findings and answered questions. We thought the issue had been concluded.

Along the way, two members of the Orange County Grand Jury visited us. The grand jury is appointed annually and consists of Orange County residents who volunteer a year of their time to hear criminal indictments brought by the district attorney and investigate local government issues. The allegation of the missing ninety-six acres had piqued their interest.

The city attorney and I first met the two grand jury members in a city hall conference room and walked them through the details of our investigation. It was clear to me that, as laypeople, they had little to no understanding of anything pertinent to the issues: land use planning, subdivision processing, park code requirements, offers of dedication, etc. After several hours in the conference room, we drove them to the Marina Hills community and the Salt Creek Corridor.

The Marina Hills community had been developed with several hundred homes, and the neighborhood parks (which comprised a small portion of the ninety-six acres) had been completed. After driving the home-lined streets, we took them to the Salt Creek Corridor, a 235-acre open space area that ran from Chapparosa Community Park to Laguna Niguel's boundary with the adjacent City of Dana Point. What seemed obvious to the city attorney and me was not as obvious to our new grand jury friends. "So where are the ninety-six acres?" they asked. "You're standing in them," we replied.

The final grand jury report was not kind to the Laguna Niguel Community Services District, the county, or Taylor Woodrow. In a series of findings and recommendations, it criticized virtually everyone involved in the subdivision review and approval process, and the quitclaim deed transaction. The district attorney announced that no criminal charges would be brought against anyone for lack of sufficient evidence of any wrongdoing. But it was the last sentence of the grand jury report that sticks in my mind to this day. Notwithstanding the district attorney's statement, the grand jury's report concluded, "We still smell a rat."

Chapter 44

─────❧❧❧─────

WHERE'S THE RENT?

THE NEW CITY of Laguna Niguel had inherited county permits that allowed several companies to place advertising bus shelters and benches on public streets. The city council initially wanted to replace these commercial advertisement structures with city-owned, non-advertising shelters and benches when the county permits expired.

After analysis, city staff concluded that the purchase and installation of city-owned shelters and benches would cost an estimated $250,000 plus ongoing maintenance costs. Instead, staff suggested that the city could earn $250,000 and obtain other community benefits by awarding an exclusive franchise to one company for the placement of advertising and non-advertising at selected locations throughout the city. The council agreed.

During the review and negotiating process, the county permits expired, and several companies stopped paying the encroachment fees. The city council chose not to press the interim fee issue to avoid creating an argument that a new or implied contract had been established. Everyone was on board, or so we thought.

I arrived at city hall one morning to discover the door to the copying room locked and the copying machine continuously operating. When the door opened, a councilmember emerged. When I asked if I could be of assistance, he replied, "Don't worry. You're really good on your feet."

Later that day, the phone calls began. The councilmember had attended a meeting of the Orange County Transportation Authority (and I think the Orange County Board of Supervisors) to question who authorizes the placement of bus shelters and bus benches on public streets and why the owners of such facilities in Laguna Niguel were enjoying the use of public streets without paying rent. I explained the situation to the newspaper reporters and advised the other city councilmembers of the antics of their mischievous colleague. I assumed the issue was over.

The next day, a Laguna Niguel newspaper's headline blared, "$24,000 Unaccounted For. Where's the Rent, Councilman Asks." I immediately called the newspaper publisher and editor to ask how such a headline and story could be printed without some confirmation or rebuttal from the mayor, city manager, or city attorney. Their response? "We never thought a city councilmember would lie to us."

Chapter 45

CASINO WORKERS
AND LAND USE PLANNING

THE CITY WAS barely nine months old, and I had just come onboard as the first permanent city manager (two interim city managers had preceded me). Seemingly unhappy with prior county land use decisions and impatiently waiting for the new city council to do something, a group of residents presented the city with a proposed Ridgeline Protection and Preservation Ordinance (RPPO) with supporting petitions and signatures.

The petitions were submitted to the Orange County Registrar of Voters for review. The signatures were counted and verified, leaving the city council with three choices: (1) Adopt the proposed ordinance without modification, (2) place the proposed ordinance before local voters for consideration at a special election, or (3) refer the proposed ordinance to city staff for analysis and a report back within thirty days. The city council opted for the latter choice.

The proposed ordinance seemed to have the benefit of some legal assistance in its drafting, but the local proponents were not particularly forthcoming about its origins. The city staff analysis concluded that the proposed ordinance, if adopted, would render over seventy privately owned ridgeline parcels undevelopable and expose the city to tens of millions of dollars in inverse condemnation liability.

A decision was made to conduct a special city council meeting in the local YMCA gymnasium and present our findings and conclusions to interested residents. It was a standing-room-only crowd. After explaining the city's limited options and potentially catastrophic financial liability, a decision was made to neither adopt the proposed ordinance nor schedule a special election. Instead, the city would file an action for declaratory relief in an effort to have the proposed ordinance deemed unconstitutional on its face.

During the course of the proceedings, the city received a letter purportedly representing the resident petitioners and condemning the city's actions to reject the ordinance and not schedule an election. Someone noticed a small, unfamiliar label on the law firm's letterhead. Our stealth work began.

After some investigation, it was discovered that the label was the symbol of a Las Vegas casino workers union. The casino workers were involved in a protracted labor dispute with a casino owner. The casino owner also owned undeveloped ridgeline property with white-water ocean views in Laguna Niguel. The proposed Ridgeline Protection and Preservation Ordinance was a scam. It was intended to prevent or complicate development of the casino owner's property. However, to avoid pinpointing its real intent, the proposed ordinance had been drafted to protect undeveloped hillside and ridgeline properties in general.

The city met with the local residents who had become the lead petitioners and proponents for the RPPO. We had to inform them that they had been duped. The city promised to initiate proceedings to draft and adopt its own Hillside Protection Ordinance. In turn, the residents agreed to enter into a stipulated judgment in favor of the city's efforts to invalidate the bogus Ridgeline Protection and Preservation Ordinance.

Chapter 46

———— ∞ ————

YOUNG MAN, YOU'RE BUSTED

NIGUEL ROAD IS a four-lane divided arterial highway that runs from Pacific Coast Highway in Dana Point to Alicia Parkway in Laguna Niguel. The segment between La Hermosa Avenue and Crown Valley Parkway is the most severe downhill portion of the road.

Shortly into my tenure as the new city manager, my executive assistant came into my office to inform me that a minicam crew and reporter were parked by the front door of city hall waiting to interview me. "About what?" I asked. "About some skateboarder that got arrested by the sheriff's department," she replied.

As a new city, Laguna Niguel did not have its own police department and contracted for law enforcement services with the Orange County Sheriff's Department. I walked outside to meet the television news reporter who confirmed that she wanted to do an on-camera interview about the "skateboarder incident." Not knowing what she was talking about, I pressed her for more information.

As it turned out, one of Laguna Niguel's more courageous youth had decided that the Niguel Road slope between La Hermosa Avenue and Crown Valley Parkway would make a great slalom run for a skilled skateboarder. Apparently, he zigzagged down the street several times making sweeping curb-to-curb turns in active traffic before one or more motorists contacted the sheriff's department. A deputy arrived on scene, arrested and handcuffed the young man, placed him in the rear seat of the patrol car, and put his skateboard in the trunk of his car. The young man was taken to the South Orange County Sheriff's Substation to await his release to his parents. Other drivers who witnessed the arrest and felt that his detention was a bit of law enforcement overkill had contacted the media.

After hearing the details from the reporter, I cobbled together what I felt was a reasonable response. "We trust our deputies to exercise their best judgment and discretion many times each day," I offered up. "In this case, however, I am sure there may have been some other options to better handle the situation."

After the interview aired on television, the response from the sheriff's department and the deputy sheriff's association was swift and clear. Both felt that I had failed to properly defend the actions of the arresting officer. Time heals all wounds, and the incident soon faded from our collective memories...or so I thought.

One day, upon returning to my office from lunch, I found an odd-shaped wrapped package on my desk. I opened it and found a beautiful new skateboard with an unusual accessory mounted on the back of the board. It was a battery-operated flashing light and siren. Fortunately, our chief of police services had a good sense of humor.

Chapter 47

ATTENTION TO DETAIL

SENIOR CITIZENS WERE instrumental in supporting the incorporation of the City of Laguna Niguel. State law encouraged maximum voter registration prior to an incorporation by offering a financial incentive. Upon incorporation, a new city's population-based share of certain revenues would be based on the actual city population or three times the number of registered voters, whichever was higher.

The Laguna Niguel Senior Citizens Club had been in place for several years and had become an active and vital organization in the community. However, the community lacked a senior center, and the club conducted its meetings in the conference room of a local bank. An opportunity was envisioned. If the senior citizens launched a successful voter registration drive that generated significant revenue for the proposed city, perhaps the first city council would consider building a senior center.

The voter registration drive was successful. Rather than receiving vehicle license fee and state gas tax revenue on the basis of the city's actual population of forty-four thousand residents, the voter registration drive yielded enough new registrants to result in an assumed city population of seventy-one thousand. That meant an additional $1 million per year in the city's coffers for ten years.

A grateful city council directed staff to identify potential locations for a new senior/community center and engage an architectural firm to prepare design and construction plans. Staff identified a suitable parcel at a prominent intersection that had been offered to the city by a major residential developer to satisfy a portion of his local park dedication requirements.

Planning ensued, construction plans and specifications were approved, competitive bids were sought, a contractor was selected, and construction was begun and completed. The end result was the beautiful fourteen-thousand-square-foot Sea Country Senior and Community Center. A center director and support staff were hired, and Sea Country Senior and Community Center was dedicated and opened to great resident fanfare. The center would be operated for the exclusive use and enjoyment of the senior citizen community from 9:00 a.m. to 4:00 p.m. on weekdays, and open to the general public for classes and special events on evenings and weekends.

Sometime before or after the center's opening, a nagging thought occurred to me. The city really did own that property, didn't we? Well, it turned out that we didn't. The property had been offered to the city (another one of those irrevocable offers of dedication), but it had not formally been accepted by action of the city council. Fortunately, irrevocable offers of dedication were generally valid for twenty-five years. We promptly corrected our oversight and had the city council accept the IOD. Life continued without missing a beat (but my heart missed a couple for sure).

Chapter 48

———✺———

THE NRA AND THE SCHOOLTEACHER

A Laguna Niguel youth had been injured in a BB gun accident. The parents wanted to know if it was lawful to possess and discharge a BB gun within city limits. Although Laguna Niguel was blessed with an abundance of open space, it was rapidly developing into a suburban bedroom community with thousands of new homes being built.

The chief of police services assured the concerned parents that BB guns were indeed illegal in the new city, but we soon discovered they were not. Upon incorporation, the city had inherited all Orange County codified ordinances. The county codes did include a prohibition on the possession and discharge of firearms within the unincorporated area, and this prohibition continued to apply within the new city limits. However, the definition of a "firearm" was tied to the definition of the same term in federal law. We were not aware that the US Congress had amended the federal definition of a firearm to exclude BB guns, pellet guns, and similar devices. We set out to amend the city's ordinance to reestablish BB guns and pellet guns as firearms subject to prohibition in the city.

On the night that the proposed ordinance amendment was to be considered by the city council, we knew something was up. Several busses had parked outside of city hall, and their passengers were starting to file into the council chambers. As we came to learn, the National Rifle Association (NRA) had recruited members from outside the city to attend the council meeting and oppose the reimposition of the BB gun prohibition.

As one person after another approached the microphone to oppose the recommended prohibition, I noticed a petite red-haired woman sitting in the audience awaiting her turn to speak. The city attorney had also noticed her and leaned over to me and said, "Looks like a schoolteacher to me. She's probably here to speak in favor of the prohibition." He was half right.

Indeed, the woman was a schoolteacher in another Orange County school district. But she was not there to support the BB gun prohibition; she had joined the others who were there to oppose the proposed ordinance. As I recall, her testimony went something like this: "I am a Laguna Niguel resident, and I own a pellet gun. After a long day at work, there's nothing I like better than to grab a beer in one hand and my pellet gun in the other and shoot at a target in my home." With that, she returned to her seat and quietly sat through the remainder of the meeting.

After lengthy testimony, the city council introduced the proposed ordinance and adopted it at the next council meeting.

P.S. The schoolteacher ran for city council at the next municipal election and was elected. She served one four-year term and did not seek reelection to a second term.

Chapter 49

———— ∞ ————

No Good Deed Goes Unpunished

THE LAGUNA NIGUEL Community Services District had a small staff of about eight to ten employees. The district had secured a good health insurance plan for small group coverage in the open commercial insurance market. Premiums were reasonable, the benefits were good, and the district board had agreed to pay the total premium cost for employees and dependents. Upon incorporation, the district's health insurance plan and premium payment policies were assumed by the city.

When I arrived as Laguna Niguel's first city manager, Julie was the receptionist/clerk at the front entrance to city hall. She answered incoming telephone calls, greeted visitors, and was the first face and voice that people encountered. However, Julie suffered from serious respiratory ailments and kept an oxygen tank next to her desk for use when necessary.

The city's health insurance plan was not pooled with other small employers. Rather, it was experience-based, which meant that premiums could rise or fall based on the number and severity of benefit claims. Unfortunately, Julie's respiratory condition worsened, and the city's health insurance premiums began to rise steeply. In a short period of time, the cost of employee and dependent coverage rose from about $250 per month to nearly $1,000 per month.

Our analysis of health insurance options offered limited choices. Given Julie's preexisting condition, no other insurance company offering comparable benefits would even give the city a quote. Kaiser Permanente, a health maintenance organization, would accept new clients, but our employees would have to exclusively use Kaiser doctors and facilities. The city council did not want to force employees to sever their personal physician relationships. A decision was made to stay with the current health insurance provider with the city continuing to pay nearly all of the escalating premium costs for employees and their families.

Ultimately, Julie's condition prevented her from working, and she retired from her position. While it was sad for everyone to see her go, her departure relieved the upward pressure on health insurance premiums. With a healthier work force, the city's premiums returned to their previous levels.

When I returned from lunch one day, I found a rubber-banded bunch of cards on my desk. They were signature cards from the Orange County Employees Association signed by most of our employees. Our employees wanted to organize.

At that time, the city was still contracting with the County of Orange for some services, including building plan check and inspection services. The county employee assigned to city hall as our deputy building official was an officer or steward of the Orange County Employees Association. He had learned of the city's new lower health insurance premiums and convinced many of our employees that they had just suffered a significant loss of "total compensation." They needed formal recognition and proper representation to fight back for the savings that the city had realized.

After several group meetings to explain our employees' rights to organize or not organize, the city adopted its first Employer-Employee Relations Resolution. The city exercised its right to determine appropriate bargaining units and established two groups: the maintenance/technical/clerical unit and the middle management/professional/supervisory unit. A group of employees who favored representation, but not necessarily by the Orange County Employees Association, formed a competing group: the Laguna Niguel Municipal Employees Association. New signature cards were circulated, and both organizations qualified for a representation election.

The city engaged the State Mediation and Conciliation Service to conduct the secret ballot representation election for each bargaining unit. The ballot choices were as follows:

1. Orange County Employees Association (OCEA)
2. Laguna Niguel Municipal Employees Association
3. No choice

A majority of the city's employees selected OCEA as the bargaining representative for both units. Good faith negotiations followed, and the city and OCEA entered into their first comprehensive memoranda of understanding covering wages, hours, and terms and conditions of employment.

As of this writing, OCEA continues to represent all employees in the maintenance/technical/clerical unit and the middle management/professional/supervisory unit.

No good deed goes unpunished.

THE MAYOR MARRIED WHO?

Chapter 50

———∞———

MISSED IT BY ONLY THAT MUCH

STARTING A NEW city from scratch is no small undertaking. Fortunately, the Laguna Niguel Community Services District had some basic infrastructure in place. Its small staff included a controller who became the city's first finance director upon incorporation. The district also had personnel rules and policies, finance policies, and an accounting system.

The Laguna Niguel Community Services District received a significant portion of the local property tax and had a multimillion-dollar fund balance. Its surplus funds were invested in the state's Local Agency Investment Fund (LAIF) and the Orange County Investment Pool (OCIP). The Orange County Investment Pool was managed by the elected county treasurer, who was considered a capable and experienced financial manager and had been in office for over twenty years. Nearly two hundred Orange County local agencies (i.e., cities, school districts, special districts, and the county itself) had deposits in OCIP.

As the new city manager, I had not given much attention to the city's investment portfolio or investment vehicles. I was familiar with LAIF from my prior city positions, but OCIP was new to me. I knew that many counties allowed other local agencies to deposit funds through their county treasurer's office and OCIP had many depositors. Its investment returns were also consistently higher than LAIF.

In 1994, the county treasurer drew an election challenger. The certified public accountant from Costa Mesa began sounding an alarm about risk in the county's investment portfolio. Although the county treasurer easily won reelection, the challenger's alarm caused the city finance director and me to take another look at the city's investments. By that time, the combined investments of the City/Laguna Niguel Community Services District had grown to $21 million. Of that amount, $3 million was deposited with LAIF and the remaining $18 million with OCIP. We agreed that we had too many eggs in the OCIP basket and began plans to diversify the portfolio.

Since all City/LNCSD funds were deposited with the state and the county, we had not established any formal relationships or accounts with investment brokers. We selected several firms and prepared to launch a new strategy. Our plan was to allocate the $21 million equally in three investments: $7 million in LAIF, $7 million in OCIP, and $7 million in US Treasury securities. We planned to seek US Treasury quotes on December 7, 1994, and complete all transactions on that day.

On December 6, 1994, one day before our planned investment transactions, Orange County declared bankruptcy. It was the largest municipality in US history ever to file for bankruptcy. The county froze the Orange County Investment Pool with $7.6 billion in deposits from local agencies. The frozen funds included the City/Laguna Niguel Community Services District's $18 million in deposited funds. The finance director and I had come within hours of better balancing and diversifying the City/LNCSD investment funds. We missed it by only that much.

Reams have been written about the reasons for the Orange County treasurer's risky investments and the county's declaration of bankruptcy. At the end of the day, the local agency depositors came close to being made whole. The City/LNCSD suffered a $900,000 loss on our $18 million in invested funds: a 5 percent haircut.

As mentioned earlier, there were only two times in my city management career when I felt that if I got fired, I deserved it. This was the second one. I kept my job.

Chapter 51

———∿∿∿———

FIVE WAYS TO KILL AN AIRPORT

MARINE CORPS AIR Station (MCAS) El Toro was the western home of Marine Corps aviation. Built in 1942, the air station occupied nearly 4,700 acres of land and included four intersecting runways: two of eight thousand linear feet and two of ten thousand linear feet. In 1993, after fifty-one years of operation, MCAS El Toro was designated for closing by the Base Realignment and Closure Commission. Its operations were transferred to Marine Corps Air Station Miramar in San Diego County, and the base officially closed in 1999.

The base closure generated considerable controversy regarding future use of the property. Many advocated for the conversion of the former air base into a major international airport. This would allow the closure of John Wayne Airport, a regional facility operated by the County of Orange. This option was strongly favored by residents of the coastal City of Newport Beach who suffered from the noise of departing aircraft from John Wayne Airport. South Orange County residents strongly objected to the idea of a major international airport. The alignment of the MCAS El Toro runways suggested that international flights arriving from the south would fly less than one thousand feet above multimillion-dollar ridgeline homes. A fierce battle was to begin.

After much pressure, the Orange County Board of Supervisors agreed to form a joint powers authority to evaluate reuse options for the air base. The El Toro Reuse Planning Authority (ETRPA) was established and included representatives from the board of supervisors and the Cities of Irvine and Lake Forest. It was agreed that ETRPA would develop three reuse plans for the base: an airport plan and two nonaviation plans.

The joint planning process was soon derailed. Commercial airport advocates qualified a ballot measure that would amend the Orange County General Plan to only allow an airport on the base property. In November 1994, Measure A passed with 51 percent of the countywide vote. Subsequently, the county withdrew from ETRPA.

The county's withdrawal from ETRPA did not dissolve the reuse planning agency. It still consisted of the Cities of Irvine and Lake Forest who invited other South Orange County cities to join. ETRPA was transformed into an airport fighting entity. The City of Laguna Niguel was staunchly opposed to the conversion of MCAS El Toro into a major international airport and assumed an active role on the ETRPA Board of Directors. As city manager, I took a lead role in the administration of ETRPA's activities, supported by two members of the City of Irvine Planning Department.

As we mapped our strategy to defeat the airport proposal, city officials and active citizens met regularly. One evening meeting was held in a hospital conference room in the City of Laguna Beach. Chaired by a councilmember from the City of Dana Point, attendees were asked to suggest ideas on how to defeat the airport proposal. When no one else volunteered, I raised my hand. "I have five ideas," I said.

When recognized, I recited my list:

1. Find a fatal flaw (i.e., financial, technical, operational, and/or environmental) in the commercial airport proposal.

2. Pursue another ballot measure to amend the Orange County General Plan to prohibit an airport use on the base property.
3. Develop a superior nonaviation alternate base reuse plan for consideration by the US Department of the Navy.
4. Elect a majority of anti-airport candidates to the Orange County Board of Supervisors.
5. Engage the county in litigation at every opportunity.

The presiding councilmember numbered and wrote each of my ideas on the whiteboard. When no other ideas were offered, he asked those in the room to vote on which idea should be pursued. I again raised my hand.

"With due respect," I began, "I don't think it's a matter of choosing one option. They all need to be pursued simultaneously." The next voice was that of the mayor of the City of Irvine. "I agree with Tim," he said. "We have to do all of them at once."

Ultimately, the commercial airport proposal was defeated. ETRPA hired a respected retired city manager to provide full-time executive leadership. His prior experience managing a city near a major international airport made him an ideal candidate to pursue our five-point strategy. ETRPA prepared the nonaviation Millennium Plan for the base, calling for a development including arts and educational institutions, a large central park, homes, and businesses. South Orange County residents actively involved themselves in other district elections for the board of supervisors, and an anti-airport majority was elected. A new ballot measure, Measure W, was circulated for signatures, certified, and placed before county voters. On March 5, 2002, Measure W was passed by a margin of 58 percent to 42 percent, amending the Orange County General Plan and eliminating the planned airport uses at MCAS El Toro.

An attempt to legally overturn Measure W failed, and the Department of the Navy adopted a nonaviation reuse plan for the base. In collaboration with the City of Irvine, the Department of the Navy and the General Services Administration announced plans to auction the base land to potential developers, including provision for a great park. In November 2003, the City of Irvine annexed the MCAS El Toro property and assumed control of its future land use planning and development.

P.S. As of this writing, the redevelopment of the former MCAS El Toro is well underway. Approximately 3,700 acres of the site are being developed with thousands of new homes, commercial uses, and schools. Thirteen hundred acres have been set aside for the Orange County Great Park. Nearly 450 acres of the park have been completed. Amenities include the Visitor's Center, the Great Park Hot Air Balloon and Children's Carousel, the 194-acre Great Park Sports Complex (championship tennis, soccer, sand volleyball, basketball, baseball, and softball facilities), the Arts Complex, and the Great Park Ice Arena. Future plans provide for a water park, concert venue, and veterans' cemetery.

Chapter 52

———∾∾∾———

WE PREFER
TO TURN THE OTHER CHEEK

THE LEGEND STARTED in 1979 with a dare and an offer of free alcohol. The Mugs Away Saloon was located on Camino Capistrano in Laguna Niguel across the street from the railroad tracks. Amtrak trains traversed the tracks several times each day traveling north and south between Los Angeles and San Diego.

On a July afternoon that year, a regular patron made an interesting proposition to other customers in the bar. He offered to buy a drink for anyone who would run outside, drop their pants, and flash their bottoms at the next passing train. Several accepted the challenge and the annual Mooning of the Amtrak ritual was born.

The annual event continued for many years. Every year on the second Saturday of July, hundreds to thousands of persons would gather at the site, press their fannies against the chain-link fence that separated the railroad tracks from the adjacent street, and moon the passing trains. Starting around 7:30 a.m. and continuing until sunset, moms, dads, kids, babies, and grandparents turned the harmless annual event into a multigenerational all-day party.

While I had never attended or observed the event, I was made aware of it before I started to work in Laguna Niguel. While wrapping things up in Redondo Beach, a greeting card arrived at my office. It was a congratulatory card for my appointment as Laguna Niguel's city manager, signed by the mayor and city council and members of the executive staff. However, the signatures on the card were unique and distinctive. Each handwritten signature had been placed within a carefully drawn derriere—all shapes and sizes—butt crack and all. That was my introduction to the Mooning of the Amtrak in Laguna Niguel.

I often wondered why the media had never contacted the city to seek its position on the annual Mooning of the Amtrak. Local newspapers covered the event each year with tasteful pictures and a related news article. In 2002, the media called. The reporter wanted to know if the city had an official position on the annual event. I was ready for him. Without missing a beat, I responded, "In Laguna Niguel, we prefer to turn the other cheek." That became the most quotable quote of my career.

Chapter 53

———— ∾∾ ————

THE MAYOR MARRIED WHO?

ON NOVEMBER 2, 2012, I officially retired from the City of Laguna Niguel after twenty-two years as its first city manager and over forty years in California city management. The recruitment and selection of my successor had not been completed, and I had agreed to stay on as interim city manager for a few months.

After a long career that included over thirty-one years as city manager in Redondo Beach and Laguna Niguel, I thought I had either heard it all, seen it all, or done it all. I was wrong.

Sometime in early 2013, my executive assistant raced into my office with a concerned look on her face. "What's wrong?" I asked. "The mayor married a woman and she can't get the marriage certificate," she replied. "What do you mean the mayor married a woman?" I questioned. "He's already married." She explained further. "No," she clarified. "He didn't marry the woman. He presided over and officiated the wedding ceremony of the woman and her groom." "Can he do that?" I asked. "I don't know," my assistant responded. "But I have the bride's mother on the line. You need to speak with her."

I picked up the transferred call and introduced myself to the woman on the line. She was a resident of the nearby City of Rancho Santa Margarita and the mother of the bride. She explained that she was a longtime friend of the mayor and had asked him to preside over the wedding ceremony of her daughter and son-in-law. The ceremony had been conducted months before, but the mayor had not provided the newlyweds with their marriage certificate. They needed it urgently because her son-in-law was about to be deployed to Afghanistan and the army needed proof of the marriage to ensure that her daughter was entitled to spousal military benefits. I listened to her carefully and promised to call her back quickly.

I promptly left my office and walked down the hall to the city attorney's office. "Terry," I asked, "did the mayor ask you if he could conduct a marriage ceremony?" "Yeah," Terry replied. "I told him that he couldn't. I gave him copies of the state code and highlighted the pertinent sections. You have to be a directly elected mayor and take a course to qualify as a wedding official." In Laguna Niguel, the mayor was appointed by the city council, not elected by the voters.

I returned to my office and called the mother of the bride. "Did the mayor tell you he was authorized to conduct the wedding ceremony?" I asked. "Yes," she replied. "He gave me some paperwork that he had received from the city attorney with some yellow highlighting on it." "Well," I continued, "I just spoke with the city attorney. I think you have the paperwork that he gave the mayor to document that he was not authorized to conduct a wedding ceremony." "Oh no," she gasped. "Does that mean that they're not legally married?" I responded, "I'm afraid so. Let me see what we can do."

Her son-in-law was scheduled to be deployed the next afternoon. With the help of my executive assistant, we contacted the Orange County Clerk-Recorder's Office, which was responsible for conducting civil marriage ceremonies and issuing marriage certificates. A deputy clerk-recorder proposed a solution. The county would void the original marriage certificate as having been lost. If the bride and groom could come to the Old County Courthouse at eight o'clock the next morning, they would be placed at the head of the line of couples waiting to be married. A civil marriage ceremony would be conducted by a qualified officiant, fees would be waived, and a marriage certificate issued. If everything went as planned, the couple would be legally married by 9:00 a.m.

I called back the mother of the bride and provided instructions. Everything went perfectly the next day. The couple was married and got to spend a few hours together before the husband's deployment overseas.

It was a memorable end to an interesting career. Kudos to the County of Orange for bending and flexing its bureaucratic rules. Kudos to my executive assistant for dropping everything she was doing that day to help put out another fire. One last time, we found a way to solve a problem and create a favorable outcome. We made three people incredibly happy and grateful that day.

ACKNOWLEDGMENTS

WELL, THAT'S IT. It's a wrap. Forty years of stories in thirty thousand words. I have a lot of people to acknowledge and thank.

To my beautiful wife, Rosalind: Thank you for your love and support. From our first date to my last day of work, you endured nearly thirty-five years of my long workdays, evening city council meetings, working weekends, and 24/7 phone calls. I can't imagine going through this crazy career with anyone but you by my side. I love you with all my heart.

To our beautiful daughter, Shannon: You have been the light of our lives. I'm sorry that I was so unavailable during the first few years of your life. I was way too focused on my career, and that is time I can never make up to you. You have blossomed into such a beautiful and wonderful woman, a loving wife to Phil, and an awesome mother to Baby Rhys. I could not be prouder of you.

To my parents (God rest their souls): Thank you for your unconditional love, support, and encouragement. You gave me free reign to pursue any and all interests and were always there to catch me when I fell. I hope I made you proud.

To Jeannie Martin: Thank you for introducing me to your dad and being a friend for these many years.

To Gayle Martin: Thank you for taking a chance on me, exciting me about the city management profession, and demonstrating the qualities and integrity of a true professional.

To Ed McCombs: Thank you for giving me my first full-time job and graciously accepting my twenty-four-hour resignation notice. I will always be grateful for that congratulatory note you sent upon my appointment as Laguna Niguel's first city manager.

To Craig Mitchell: Thank you for bailing me out and providing me with a new job at Marineland of the Pacific after my hasty departure from the City of Ventura.

To Bob Riley: Thanks for tracking me down upon my return to the South Bay and inviting me to attend and observe a Redondo Beach City Council meeting. It was a chance for a second beginning to a career I was destined to pursue.

To Dave Dolter: Thanks for the perverse promotional incentive and for convincing me to take the bird in the hand rather than wait for the bird in the bush. Accepting the assistant city manager position turned out to be one of the best choices of my career.

To the 1981 Redondo Beach City Council: Thanks for taking a chance on the thirty-one-year-old kid.

To the inaugural Laguna Niguel City Council: Thanks for taking a chance on the thirty-nine-year-old man. I really am glad that I came to work for the City of Laguna Niguel and not the City of Laguna Beach.

To all of the mayors, city councilmembers, and city staff: It was a pleasure to work with each and every one of you, and I will be forever grateful for your support.

To all city managers/administrators, deputies, and assistants: It has been my pleasure to consider myself your professional peer. You have inspired me in countless ways. Keep up the good work. Your cities and communities depend on you.

CPSIA information can be obtained
at www.ICGtesting.com
Printed in the USA
BVHW052114291222
655251BV00005BA/110

9 781977 228338